Beyond Dropping Out

Beyond Dropping Out

Overcoming the Pitfalls of School Culture

William H. Warring Jr.

ROWMAN & LITTLEFIELD
Lanham • Boulder • New York • London

Published by Rowman & Littlefield
A wholly owned subsidiary of The Rowman & Littlefield Publishing Group, Inc.
4501 Forbes Boulevard, Suite 200, Lanham, Maryland 20706
www.rowman.com

Unit A, Whitacre Mews, 26-34 Stannary Street, London SE11 4AB

Copyright © 2016 by William H. Warring Jr.

All rights reserved. No part of this book may be reproduced in any form or by any electronic or mechanical means, including information storage and retrieval systems, without written permission from the publisher, except by a reviewer who may quote passages in a review.

British Library Cataloguing in Publication Information Available

Library of Congress Cataloging-in-Publication Data

ISBN 978-1-4758-2099-7 (cloth : alk. paper) -- ISBN 978-1-4758-2100-0 (pbk. : alk. paper) -- ISBN 978-1-4758-2101-7 (electronic)

∞ ™ The paper used in this publication meets the minimum requirements of American National Standard for Information Sciences Permanence of Paper for Printed Library Materials, ANSI/NISO Z39.48-1992.

Printed in the United States of America

To Harold and Olivia Curran, who together,
made my life whole and complete

Contents

Preface	ix
Acknowledgments	xi
Introduction	xiii

I: Strengthening Schoolwide Mind-sets

1 Defeating Schoolwide Adversity 1
    Overcoming School, Program, and Classroom Struggles
    Upsetting Self-Debasement
    Efficacious Moments and Events
    Summary

2 Overcoming Roadblocks 7
    Cultural Conflict: A Continuation School Challenge
    Attribution Theory: The Blame Game
    Enhancing School Culture
    Summary

3 Trust: A Strengths-Based Asset 19
    Trusting Adult Stakeholders
    Trusting Choice
    Respect: A Foundational Asset
    Assets and Outcomes: Student Growth Development
    Summary

4 Generating College and Career Readiness 29
    Identifying College and Career Requirement Indicators
    Synthesizing Indicators with Common Core Standards
    Assessing Growth

Summary

II: Augmenting Formidable and Arduous Learning

5 Strengthening School Design   39
    Developing Program Design
    Roadblocks and Challenges
    Questioning Design
    Connectedness: A Strength-Based Protective Factor
    Addressing Student Needs
    Strengthening Teaching
    Summary

6 Interventions and Methodologies   55
    Methodologies
    Instructional Design Criteria
    Student Misbehavior Strategies
    A Multiple Pathways Approach to Curriculum Design
    Summary

7 Classroom Engagement   71
    Self-Determination: A Sense of Autonomy
    Personalizing Instruction
    Flow: A Motivational Strategy
    Restructuring Curriculum
    Effective Teaching Approaches
    Summary

III: Measuring Achievement

8 Assessing Growth   87
    Dominant Consorts
    Predicting Student Struggles
    Assessing Student Performance
    Demonstrating Assessment Tools and Strategies
    Summary

9 Laquitta and Jonathan   95

References   107

Index   117

About the Author   123

Preface

Sem Yeto High School's success attracted visitors from alternative school developers and stakeholders throughout California. It was built upon a school design allowing students to choose their classes each period of each day. Students knew what coursework they needed to graduate and the school trusted them to earn credits where and when they needed them. Although students were responsible for minimum weekly attendance and progress requirements, they satisfied those requirements on their own terms.

Students became resilient by being trusted . . . trusted to choose . . . and for many, choosing to graduate.

Academic achievement, however, was another concern.

Learning wasn't expected. Typical of continuation schools, Earning to Graduate replaced Learning to Graduate. Credits and/or credit points became the awards, replacing evidence of student learning growth. After all, everyone knew that they were *those kids* who went to *that school*, a theme that finally sealed the fate of Sem Yeto High School.

And the tradition continues.

Today, less than 20 percent of California's continuation schools offer what Deidra Kelly (1993) calls a Safety Net quality, a feature that demonstrates a school's ability to keep kids from falling through the cracks by providing them with resilient program interventions. Sem Yeto was such a school. California's Legislative Analyst's Office (LAO) in 2007 found Kelly's findings unchanged. Eighty percent of the state's continuation schools, in one fashion or another, are evidenced as harmful to children.

Amazingly, in my role as continuation school evaluator (aka *field expert*) for the California Department of Education, I have yet to uncover even a Safety Net school that prepares kids for college, career readiness, or any other form of responsible goal other than increasing graduation rates.

Lehr, Lanners, and Lange (2003) tell us that 10,900 public alternative schools and programs serve approximately 1.3 percent of the nation's public school children. Somewhere just under 1 million American schoolchildren attend continuation schools considered to be underperforming in some sort of state of *benign neglect*. These findings threaten the very survival of our nation's primary dropout intervention high school programs.

Sem Yeto closed at the finish of the spring semester of 2015. Former district leadership converted the school from its *trust-to-choose* model to a decoupled design attempting to emulate a comprehensive high school, lacking accountability. The results, predictably, sealed the school's fate. To meet California's requirement that all districts are to establish and maintain continuation programs, Sem Yeto High has become a set of classrooms located out of the way, somewhere on one or more of the district's comprehensive high school campuses.

No one knows what to do with *those kids* who go to *those schools*.

This work attempts to replace frustrating attitudes commonly held by educational stakeholders with well-cited efforts, experiences, and foundational evidence successful at effecting school change. It is sincerely hoped that this work's resources will further enhance and expand the many benefits they bring to our schools and classrooms. Our kids deserve no less.

Acknowledgments

Judy Edwards, an outstanding continuation high school teacher during Sem Yeto High School's golden years, taught me not only the academics of English but also effective engagement strategies for struggling writers and readers as well. She motivated me, supported me, and filled me with hope for continuation students everywhere.

Mike Jines and Ken Lowe, two of Sem Yeto's award-winning high school teachers, showed me how to make subject matter relevant to continuation students' lives through assessment-driven pedagogy. And Sem Yeto's principal, Dick Chadwick, not only provided me with a unique and effective educational experience that defined my K–12 teaching career but also showed me the value of patience, understanding, and responsibility.

I once again wish to acknowledge Scott Griffith, EdD; Angel Rivera, MA, MS; Mike Ilic, EdD; Mary K. Carlon; Cintia Quinn; and my wonderful wife, Diane, for their help and support during these past four years.

These are but a handful of influences whose outstanding careers and efforts have affected this work. Each and every one supported me in assembling the constructs, pedagogies, evidence, and experiences found herein, program development characteristics that support thinkers and practitioners who are sincerely concerned about our nation's most vulnerable high-schoolers, those at risk of dropping out.

Introduction

Alternative (continuation) schools throughout the country must increase not only their overall educational capacities but their student performance levels as well. Their survivals require it. This work attempts to convince schools that no matter the struggles their student populations face, all hold capacities to achieve at rigorous levels, regardless of the current and future outlooks held by their students and stakeholders.

By first identifying, then using protective factors found among and within a school's student attributes, a resilient continuation school will enable itself to launch student achievement levels to unimaginable heights—heights allowing formidable higher-education successes and career-level accomplishments. By using schoolwide protective factors to reduce the effects of student adversities, continuation students encounter significant opportunities never before realized.

The more protective factors (*assets*) of a school, the more resilient a school's potential. As such, schoolwide resiliency must be directly related to student achievement. Parents, districts, and communities expect and deserve it.

***

The material provided herein is the result of evidence leading to conclusions provided by research-based study. It offers changers an array of choices in which to construct or improve upon alternative programming and classroom designs to prepare students not only for college and career readiness but also for futures filled with capacities exceeding existing K–12 frameworks.

Changers deserve choice, and this work attempts to provide constructs, experiences, opinions, and evidence, in which they can pair their school's challenges with their own personal educational values to significantly strengthen student achievement.

***

Continuation schools, classes, and programs are represented by two descriptors—*alternative* and *continuation*—throughout this work. All student narratives represented herewith are based upon actual events with names being fictionalized to protect student anonymity.

Academic and career-level achievements born from effective schools are derived from the findings, opinions, interactions, and conclusions of authors and researchers supporting three growth domains: strengthening schoolwide mind-sets, augmenting student learning, and measuring achievement. It is the intent of this work to demonstrate that program developers and changers can grow alternative school and student achievement through synthesizing theory, research, practice, and hope.

A complete list of statewide policies and legislations affecting alternative education are provided by Lehr, Lanners, and Lange (2003) and can be found at: http://files.eric.ed.gov/fulltext/ED502533.pdf.

I

Strengthening Schoolwide Mind-sets

Chapter One

Defeating Schoolwide Adversity

Students suffering from the consequences of adversity bring mind-sets to schools and classrooms very much different from those of their teachers and staff. The differences most often conflict with one another, showing themselves in student failure. Struggles and hardships emerging from the fragmented recesses of students' family conditions differ as well with conditions alternative students see in the lives of others. The confusion leads to a vulnerability in student mind-sets.

"There are points of reorganization in a life course," however, "at which a [student's] vulnerability or resiliency to particular environments might change," say Werner and Smith (1992), due to varying *protective factors* adopted by individual students (pp. 4–5).

Protective factors block discord that perpetuates adversity, thereby increasing self-esteem and efficacy, two necessary growth attributes.

***

Ellis and Harper (1997) provide a pedagogical framework offering a wide range of student achievement protective factors. The researchers suggest that as we accept attitudes and beliefs, we build self-imposed *thought* frameworks—frameworks that when challenged promote powerful feelings. Feelings cultivate action or behaviors that can readily be evaluated. The resulting evaluation criteria confirms or alters the attitude and belief framework. Simply put, as our beliefs are challenged, feelings are created that cause us to react in ways that either alter or accept existing attitudinal frameworks.

The challenge creates movement in a three-point wheel or cycle that appears as a challenged belief creating feelings that provoke action. The results of the action (or behavior) either support the belief or alter it, allowing for either acceptance for the status quo or change.

When change is sought, it is found that among the three points, challenging *attitude* is more effective than attempting to challenge feelings or behavior. When thought is challenged, feelings ignite images of behaviors that foresee an outcome most likely generated by the thought. A quick assessment allows the thinker to either build or extinguish the thought, depending upon his or her want or need.

It also offers opportunities at challenging not only student mind-sets, but mind-sets held by schools and programs as well.

OVERCOMING SCHOOL, PROGRAM, AND CLASSROOM STRUGGLES

School and subsequent home visits provide overwhelming evidence of powerlessness held by many alternative school families. Many survive moment to moment, encumbered by family histories of failure and loss. Behaviors generated by feelings created by these beliefs are brought into classrooms, often absorbed by faculties and staffs who, unknowingly, continue perpetuating adversity into their schools through programming and curriculum.

***

Continuation teachers are noticeably unsettled when discussing student struggles. Teachers most often appear lost and confused when analyzing common core standards and their relationships to alternative student frustrations. They argue the values of *effort* while avoiding discussion of student *learning*.

Alternative teachers commonly award credits for class attendance and assignment completion. Students and staff are united in understanding that credits lead to diplomas. Diplomas come from credit gathering rather than learning, an anomaly resulting in a lacking state of college and career readiness.

"I believe they're incapable [attitude] which frustrates me [feeling] when I try to teach them," commented one member of a continuation faculty room discussion. "So I give them assignments out of workbooks [behavior] that most don't turn in anyway. See? Like I said before, they're just not capable. I don't even know why we try" [confirmed attitude] . . . and the cycle continues.

***

Programs develop attitudes. And once resilient attitudes overcome adversity, effective schoolwide programs emerge from accelerating student assessments—assessments that generate purposeful, effective school settings, and settings that perpetuate strong, high levels of student learning. Resilient attitudes that perpetuate effective schoolwide programs produce schools that overcome unyielding change resistance, a pathway to overcoming the odds.

UPSETTING SELF-DEBASEMENT

She lived in a room on the second floor of a worn-down motel with her two brothers, mother, and stepfather. It was located on the back of a vacant, weed-infested lot separating it from a local car dealer. Constant police patrols, looking for drug dealing and subsequent paraphernalia, continually harassed her by asking how she was earning her spare money. Her family lived there rent-free as compensation for her stepfather serving as the motel handyman. She was sixteen.

Every twenty-eight days, the motel manager moved her family to a different room, an act necessary to sidestep a state law requiring a thirty-day notice to evict under a month-to-month tenancy. The manager didn't trust whether or not the handyman's drinking or other concerns might require him to throw him and his family out.

She knew another reality, however. It seems the manager made her aware of a desire he quietly held for her. His flirting took precedence over her stepfather's drunkenness, making her skills at keeping him at arm's length a primary factor in her family's housing concerns. School provided her with a long-term avoidance strategy, one she used to its fullest.

One afternoon while sitting in her fifth-period class, she slid from her chair onto the floor, unconscious. After being rushed to a nearby hospital, a student quietly turned in an essay he found on her desk. It told of a belief she held, one claiming that if she upset her manager's advances, his anger would cause her family's eviction, yet agreeing to his advances was unconscionable. She held herself responsible for her family's housing concerns. Her advisor offered help.

During a lunch discussion, her advisor learned of other responsibilities she assumed, parental responsibilities ignored by her mother and stepfather. He asked her about her brothers, how well they were doing, and whether or not they held any responsibilities. They did not. He furthered his questions about her personal hopes and dreams and whether or not she felt them possible. She did not. He finally asked her if her family could survive without her help and support. She replied, they could not.

Her beliefs were held firmly. So her advisor quizzed her about any other responsibilities she believed she had regarding her stepfather's drunkenness or her mother's apathetic condition. She responded with a confusing nod. He asked her if she would join him in an activity that might help rid her of her state of morosity.

He asked her to write a paragraph describing in detail a moment when she achieved at something beyond her hopes and dreams, a moment when she felt being in a state of omnipotence. The description needed to include the most minute details of her experience, enhanced by descriptions of her feelings. She was then asked to follow up with another absolute belief statement: "I like myself . . . I like myself unconditionally and I am now experiencing . . . " (a detailed description of her benefitting from something she wants).

He told her to write it as if she was living the experience right now, in the present.

He provided her with a pocket-sized tape recorder to record her paragraphs in her own voice so she could play them back as often as she chose. The recordings made her feel strong, powerful and complete, feelings resulting in activities that abruptly stopped the manager's harassments and provided her an avenue for healthy housing for her and her family. They provided her with a pathway to graduation. Her advisor last learned that she was helping her parents make their own tapes, tapes that would allow them to overcome their own personal struggles.

EFFICACIOUS MOMENTS AND EVENTS

Student self-efficacy as a student growth category fits well into Ellis and Harper's three-point cycle of challenged attitudes, creating feelings that in turn, motivate behavior, behavior that supports, adjusts, or replaces original attitudes.

Interestingly, however, is the manner in which alternative students visualize their beliefs. It's almost as if they see them through a diverse lens. A Northern California study involving five continuation schools in five districts asked resilient students to identify moments or events occurring in their lives, critical incidents that altered their behaviors, leading them toward graduation (Warring, 2011). For the most part, student participants responded with vigor, detailing incidents that influenced their resiliencies with sincerity and trust.

Resilient continuation students were asked, "Did anything happen in your life that influenced you so much, it led you to believe that you really can graduate? If so, what was it?" A *critical incident* was described by one student as a *spark* of understanding. Student sparks included:

"My advisor said it's really easy. Just do what the teachers say and all that. Just tell yourself everyday that's what you want to do and do it."

"I'm in a program called Second Chance. My teachers inspired me and told me that I can pull up from where I was and do good. When I clean up my act and do everything I'm supposed to do, I'll be on track to graduate. That caused me to realize I have a chance . . . I really can graduate."

"During third period, it hit me that teachers here present the material in a way I thought about it . . . you know, in my head. For the first time ever, I get it!"

"Extra credit and going to school made me realize I might really make it. I decided to stay after school instead of hanging around friends that's not getting me anything. My advisor went over how many credits I had left. Oh my god. It really motivated me."

"We have to carry our transcripts around in our binders. Our advisors make us. Every quarter, we get new transcripts with our new credits on them. I got motivated when I saw how few credits I still needed. Look! See? It says right here. That means I can graduate on time at the end of this year. I'll be the first one in my family. That'll turn anybody on."

Efficacy growth appeared to come from more than critical incidents, however. One student told the interviewer,

> One school passed me off and this one told me I could graduate, maybe even early if I tried hard enough. That's all. It was that simple. Awesome. I was just one of the failures and now I'm one of the very best . . . each one of us means something to somebody . . . know what I mean?

SUMMARY

Mind-sets held by students living in adversity most often differ from their teachers and staff members. The conflicting differences are often seen in student failure. Protective factors created by the students block many of their struggles and may well increase their self-esteems and efficacies, two attributes necessary for growth.

Ellis and Harper (1997) provide a pedagogical framework offering a wide range of student achievement protective factors. The researchers suggest that as we accept attitudes and beliefs, we build self-imposed *thought* frameworks; frameworks that when challenged promote powerful feelings. Feelings cultivate behaviors that confirm or alter attitude and belief frameworks.

The team's framework serves as an improvement model for alternative education settings.

Change occurs as attitudes and beliefs are challenged. Rewriting self messages adjusts harmful feelings, allowing for a student, program, or school to promote responsible behaviors or actions. Teachers, however, are mostly frustrated by a majority of continuation student educational adversities, adversities that can be overcome by changing mind-sets.

Once resilient mind-sets overcome adversity, effective schoolwide programs emerge from accelerating student assessments, assessments that generate purposeful, effective school settings, settings that perpetuate strong, high levels of student learning. Resilient mind-sets that perpetuate effective schoolwide programs produce schools that overcome unyielding change resistance.

Student, program, and schoolwide efficacy fit well into a cycle of challenged attitudes, creating feelings that in turn motivate behavior—behavior that supports, adjusts, or replaces originally held attitudes. Change simply requires another look at challenging stakeholder beliefs.

Chapter Two

Overcoming Roadblocks

She stood just under five feet, six inches, with a string of orange hair dangling loosely over her right eye. Her freckles intensified the blue in her eyes while highlighting a pinkness in her cheeks. Hansen's presence most often enlightened others, so as she stood outside the principal's office stooped and wanting, fighting back tears, friends surrounded her, holding her, hugging her.

"I don't get it," she mumbled. "Is all this just bullshit? I worked my ass off all year long. I earned all my credits . . . okay, except algebra. I signed up for summer school to finish that. I knew I couldn't graduate with my class in June and now look . . . look what the principal just gave me."

She held up her fresh, new diploma, showing it to her friends. They gasped.

Hansen learned the power of her father's position within the school district. Even though her algebra teacher and father were unaware, the principal signed off on Hansen's final five algebra credits, allowing her to walk with her graduating class. The principal truly believed he was doing the right thing for Hansen and her family. After all, she was a wonderful student and deserved support on those rare occasions when she needed it.

Hansen, on the other hand, believed that *earning* and *respect* were synonymous and that her abilities, therefore her person, were disrespected when the principal granted her diploma. She said the principal's action taught her that she wasn't capable of earning her final algebra credits since he had to give them to her. Hansen worried that she had been disrespected by others she admired most at school. When a thought suggested that success in her other courses might also be influenced by the same perceptions, she broke into tears. No one at her school ever saw her again. She never walked with her class.

***

An alternative school culture described as being in a state of *benign neglect* requires significant change, beginning with its foundation—a school's bedrock depicted by its traditions, beliefs, policies, and norms that can be shaped, enhanced, and maintained through the school's site leadership. And traditions, beliefs, policies, and norms within an effective continuation school reveal a foundational building block known as *respect*.

As Hansen's experience has shown, disrespecting any schoolwide policy or rule, no matter the argument(s), can destroy *trust* in a school's cultural tradition, exposing yet a second critical cornerstone embedded in a strong foundation.

Faculty room discussions are often absent a third determinative building block, *student growth*, an assumed outcome of schoolwide trust leading to respect. Interviews with continuation students suggest that schoolwide respect demands a schoolwide relevant and rigorous curriculum.

A common assumption among continuation faculties, however, is that their students lack capacity, forcing rigor to be fruitless. Attempts to avoid damaging student self-esteems have created a lowering of curriculum standards in many alternative schools, even among those considered as *safety-net* schools. Practitioner Q&A discussions have consistently shown that rigor is believed to breed failure among continuation students, resulting in increased dropout rates. Resilient students become lost and confused.

***

School visits confirm that coursework lacking relevance and rigor is built upon external rewards, often referred to as *points* or *credit points* (aka, units awarded to assignment completion), that lead to credits resulting in high school graduation. By concentrating on completing the work rather than absorbing the curricula, students avoid, if not ignore, academic learning while seeking an array of credits leading to their diplomas.

Resilient students argue, therefore, that their continuation diplomas are less valuable than those awarded comprehensive high school graduates. Curriculum-based learning is replaced by a credit-point schoolwide economy rewarding students for attending school and simply doing their work.

Continuation students are not offered the rigorous curricular opportunities found in their feeder or comprehensive schools, a condition often questioned by resilient continuation students. "Possibly the most attractive argument for insisting on algebra and geometry for all students," says Noddings (2003), "is that *equality of opportunity* demands it" (p. 201).

CULTURAL CONFLICT: A CONTINUATION SCHOOL CHALLENGE

States provide alternative education programs for those often living within and among blighted living conditions, struggling with perpetual hunger, and who are, at best, vulnerable to lack of health care access, resulting in poor physical and emotional health.

One in five comprehensive students bring these living conditions to school each day along with an indeterminable number of alternative students. Schoolwide at-risk factors are furthered with continuation students so often suffering from literacy and language development adversities and lacking economic resources, and they have inconsistent mobilities and diverse expectations, values, and beliefs separating home and school.

***

Teachers are often frustrated with seemingly invisible student handicaps often misdiagnosed as student discontent or *laziness*. Studies, however, expose the effects of cultural adversity on vulnerable students at all capacity levels and in all subject areas. Parrett and Budge (2012) suggest, "More than 50 years of research indicates that children who are poor hear a smaller number of words with more limited syntactic complexity and fewer conversation-eliciting questions, making it difficult for them to quickly acquire new words" (p. 119).

A cultural conflict divides large numbers of students living in economically adverse conditions from mostly white, middle-class teachers who struggle as they try to understand why their students don't want what they want them to have. In the light of classrooms filled with such diversity, a teacher might wonder how any school, alternative or otherwise, can or should prepare students for teacher-held perceptions of healthy futures.

***

As arguments surround academic achievement levels necessary for K–12 student success, a need for a basic foundation of academic capability arises. All students must learn the academic basics. Schools have a responsibility to provide the same opportunities for those born into affliction as are offered those more fortunate. Failure to meet this responsibility is shown by companies frustrated by job applicants academically unprepared for training in career positions.

Corporate and business needs for skilled, educated workers continue growing alongside American high school dropout rates:

> Corporate CEOs in the U.S. report that lower corporate earnings estimates were caused partly by a shortage of skilled workers. In 1992, only 27% reported this type of negative economic impact caused by the poor skills of workers; by 1995, almost half reported the problem, and by 1998, almost 70% of the CEOs indicated that company earnings would be lower because of workers' educational defects. About half of the CEOs surveyed said they were unsatisfied with the quality of job applicants. "Public education today," according to William Brock, former U.S. Secretary of Labor, "is totally inadequate to the task. Our schools are not designed for the workplace." (Nelson, Palonsky, & McCarthy, 2007, p. 203)

American career opportunities for undereducated, latent adolescents are extremely rare, with many arguing they no longer exist. Jobs filled by previous generations have moved to foreign countries and cultures where earning opportunities are reported as being highly appreciated and respected. Labor outsourcing has filled our nation's business and industrial needs as our unemployed dropouts evidence the results.

Internationally, synthesized economies are hiring the world's poor who are most often without governmental protection or representation. Many international companies hiring practices are free from government intervention. Foreign labor competition has created a lack of American capacity to produce livable economic opportunities. And the futures of the undereducated become even bleaker.

The U.S. Census Bureau (2000) found:

> During the last half of the twentieth century, the proportion of farmers and farm workers has declined from almost 20% of the workforce to only 3% while manufacturing jobs have declined from about 32% to 27%. The most prominent change has been in the kinds of jobs available with service jobs increasing from about 53% to 69%. White-collar jobs rose from about 45% of the labor force in 1940 to over 70% by the mid-1980's and about 80% by 2000. Blue-collar jobs declined from about 42% to about 20% over the same period. (in Nelson, Palonsky, & McCarthy, 2007, pp. 200–1)

The Bureau states that schools are central to an effective, secure, and responsible development of our American economy, which it argues requires a well-educated populace. Simply put, nations are in a race in terms of expanding and improving their educational systems. Continuation schools cannot be exempt. There are no *alternative colleges* or *continuation career* opportunities. Continuation students deserve more than a diploma.

ATTRIBUTION THEORY: THE BLAME GAME

Attribution theory offers a framework for understanding how motivation affects achievement. Understanding the tenet allows for overcoming both student and family roadblocks to academic growth. Recurring discontent between parents and schools fashions a *blame game*, blaming *those people* who work in *those schools* for student failure.

Belief systems held by those on hard times are commonly observed in alternative classroom settings. Parents of at-risk students are more than aware of college prep courses, AP classes, and school activities common to students other than their own. Discussions demonstrate seemingly apathetic concerns. It's almost as if there's an acceptance of *those people* who go to *those schools* simply being better than their kids. Divergent opportunities shared by cultural inequities, both in and out of schools, are well hidden.

Alternative school parents carefully and most often internally question why schools allow the unfairness. Left with little choice, families are known to explain their children's school histories, both to themselves and others, by attributing *cause* to their circumstances. "We're this way because my boyfriend left me with these kids so he can go smoke up my child support. I do my best with no help. I have to. Who else's gonna take care of these kids?"

Seligman (1990) suggests that blaming others offers a greater sense of control, with *control* being a necessary *respect* attribute. "Respect," a dominant feature sought by many living with so little, is earned through behaviors of others, and as such, strongly affects self-esteems held by those living within and among adversity. Behavioral explanations, according to Seligman, are seen as effective determiners for measuring respect levels among those many.

He teaches two attribution behaviors important to first understanding, then implementing, a blame-game reversion. According to blamers, when someone else has erred, an *internal attribution* is the cause of the error, saying it is most often due to his or her internal personality factors. A personal error, on the other hand, exemplifies an *external attribution*, attributing causes to situational factors to avoid blaming oneself. When success is discussed, the one committing the mistake reverses the attributions, attributing his or her successes internally and the successes of any rivals to external luck.

***

Student's emotional and motivational drives can drive attributions. Blaming others so as to avoid personal recrimination is a *self-serving attribution*. Students with high needs to avoid failure tend to make attributions that put themselves in a good light. Blaming creates beliefs and attitudes that attribute consequences to events—events never seen by a blamer as a personal fault.

Factors commonly causing those living among adverse conditions to attribute consequences to events include:

- whether or not the outcome can be attributed to a controllable or uncontrollable cause or event
- whether the outcome is attributed to a stable or variable cause
- whether or not the outcome is attributed to an internal or external source. (Weiner, 2000, in Boykin & Noguera, 2011, p. 259)

The first factor questions whether or not students or families believe they control their abilities to arrive at outcomes or if they feel it is due to factors beyond their control. The second looks at whether outcomes occur constantly or fluctuate over time, and the final addresses whether or not the outcome is attributed to something within the student or from a surrounding environment.

"For nearly 40 years," say Boykin and Noguera (2011), "attribution theory has been an influential framework for understanding how motivation affects achievement. People seek explanations for events [and their consequences] in which they have participated" (p. 61).

***

Two attributions that help understand achievement differences as well as raise performance outcomes are the notions of ability and effort. Ability lies at the intersection of relatively uncontrollable, stable, and internal causes, whereas effort lies at the intersection of controllable, variable, and external causes. Ability attributions convert into enduring beliefs that students hold about their prospects for success and failure in school, whereas effort attributions are more strongly related to adaptive achievement outcomes.

Simply put, a student's sense of ability defines his or her capacity, and is therefore unchangeable. An effort, however, is most often seen as adapting to requirements necessary to get whatever a student wants. While *ability* is unchangeable and therefore oppressive, *effort* allows choice, which provides awareness.

Studies are currently looking at how these different outcomes have become a function of student and family beliefs. Ways of altering those beliefs are also being looked at as researchers study learning strategies emphasizing effort, rather than ability. Implicit theories, those not necessarily held consciously, are used as foundations for looking at how students and families see the natures of their abilities that create self-beliefs (Blackwell, Trzesniewski, & Dweck, 2007; Dweck & Leggett, 1988; Molden & Dweck, 2006).

Understanding these theories moves participants from a condition of self-doubt to one focusing on effort, a movement leading to learning opportunities.

While an entity, or fixed view, alongside *ability focusing* stagnates effort, incremental or malleable viewpoints hold that such attributes are open to change. They can improve or expand one's competence or intelligence. Malleable viewpoints offer opportunities at reversing blame games.

***

Merari's father sees no need for her staying in school. She's needed to help in the family restaurant. No one in his family ever graduated anyway. Work, that's what matters. That's what feeds families. The family cannot afford Merari hanging around some school to get a diploma that doesn't pay any bills.

Mr. Ramos, one of Merari's teachers, took special interest in her plight. He had been invited into conversations involving her struggles and had read numerous essays addressing her throes, enough to realize her father nurtures blame games.

He began by looking into Merari's family culture, primarily her father's. Mr. Ramos understood a fatherly duty inherent in Hispanic families, but a sense of control isn't necessarily tied to duty and is often motivated by fear. He needed to discover attributions affecting the father's influence over Merari's decision to either graduate or drop out. To do so, he needed time with Merari's father—significant time, time enough to acquire respect.

He wanted to learn of any internal causes affecting her father's lack of support for her graduation, any external causes attributing to his efforts as well as anything attributing to his attitudes about Merari's education. Might they be fixed or malleable?

Mr. Ramos dropped by the restaurant after school, when business was slow. He would not address nor discuss his awareness of Merari's graduation struggles. He had far better results when he reversed an active blame game. Merari's father showed proper respect for Mr. Ramos's visit by placing a pair of beers on an isolated table at the far end of his restaurant's seating area. He nodded to Mr. Ramos, signifying an invitation to sit. As both sipped the foam from the tops of their mugs, Merari's father agreed to speak in English.

"Señor Reyes," Mr. Ramos began. "Merari, as you know, is a remarkable young lady devoted to you and your family. I know these things because she boasts about all of you in her essays. She is very proud . . . proud of you, her mom, and her brothers and sister. She says so. She wants to devote her life to you and her family, so much so that she is thinking about dropping out of school so she can help here in the restaurant."

Mr. Reyes's eyes lit up.

Mr. Ramos ignored the response and dropped his head. He whispered, "So I need your help. Her decision to leave school could cost your family thousands of dollars; money you could well use to support your restaurant, take care of your other children and provide for you and your wife when you retire."

Merari's father frowned in confusion.

"It's simple," Mr. Ramos continued. "Merari's natural school abilities motivate her to study and study hard. She knows things, Mr. Reyes, things that can graduate her from high school and beyond. She is committed to you and her family, and as an accountant, business woman, or attorney, she can provide so much more to your restaurant and household than she can now. You've done a remarkable job with her, sir, and you deserve the benefits that come from such a wonderful daughter."

"Frankly, Mr. Reyes, I need your help in convincing her not only to stay in school, but to continue on as well." Mr. Ramos sparked a respect from Merari's father, one creating a relationship that has lasted far beyond Merari's graduation from high school, college, and a well-respected Midwestern business school.

ENHANCING SCHOOL CULTURE

Enhancing school culture is directly tied to a school's success in strengthening cultural characteristics that describe its own personal character. A continuation school's character can be supplemented by analyzing its student learning successes as evidenced by the school's research-based, assessment procedures.

Waters (2011) finds that positive cultural change within a school requires school staff to not only learn new skills and techniques but also to reexamine what are often deeply held beliefs about student learning and how school professionals should work. These strong cultural growth attributes produce two high-performing school qualities, *relevance* and *rigor*, both known to improve the qualities of student learning while reducing variances of teaching quality.

***

Relevance and rigor are attracting significant educational attention. These two constructs not only revise and reinforce student self-respect, they also promote student self-efficacy that exceeds the wants and needs of a resilient continuation school culture (Warring, 2011). They build upon a school's academic optimism, making visible a third construct known as *academic press*: "the behavioral aspect of academic optimism which is the extent to which a school is driven by academic excellence" (Hoy, Tarter, & Woolfolk-Hoy, 2007, in Hoy & DiPaola, eds., 2009, pp. 79–80).

Academic press is seen in schoolwide involvements with national honor societies as well as students entering local academic competitions such as student debates and mock trials. "[Continuation] teachers need to believe that both they and their students are up for the challenge of high student achievement by first respecting, then celebrating the school's [academic] honor roll students," say Hoy and Tarter's study group.

***

While district leaderships tell faculties to adhere to a resiliency theory allowing that all students can learn, frustrated continuation folks often ask, "Learn what and from whom?" Faculties struggle with these two questions while realizing that professional development opportunities and educational resources advancing alternative education are for the most part severely lacking. The struggles persist as adverse continuation school cultural components outweigh compliances with academic press that in turn perpetuate conflict.

Frustrations compound as students continue their graduation struggles. They need and deserve teachers who build upon their strengths to improve their academic weaknesses—who relieve pressure with support, and are knowledgeable not just about their subject matter but also about how to help struggling, alternative students learn (Ruiz de Velasco, April 2008). Students not only need personal help through rigorous courses, they need to believe in their efforts . . . that they're worth it.

The Character Education Partnership, in its position paper, *Developing and Assessing School Culture: A New Level of Accountability for Schools*, describes a positive school culture as including "the school-wide ethos and the culture of individual classrooms, high expectations for learning and achievement, a safe and caring environment, shared values and relational trust, a powerful pedagogy and curriculum, high student motivation and engagement, a professional faculty culture, and partnerships with families and the community" (p. 1).

***

It is argued that education must look outside its paradigm for change components necessary to significantly increase achievement outcomes. Nelson, Palonsky, and McCarthy (2007) take the position that schools are currently inefficient. They could well benefit from adopting cultural as well as operational business models. "Unlike educational paradigms, corporations have made remarkable progress in building efficiency and productive gains. . . . Private enterprise cannot survive stagnation and as such, U.S. industries have avoided growth stoppage. . . . Improved technology and productivity could increase school efficiency considerably" (p. 209).

Competition forces businesses to readjust and reorganize while consistently assessing the effectiveness of their cultural traits, primarily their practices. Schools should not be exempt from similar requirements, argue Nelson's study group.

A generational conflict continues, however, between attitudes held by both education and business paradigms. Informal discussions with practitioners representing both concerns suggest that business personnel most often see themselves as incapable of dealing with educational challenges, and teachers do not want those in their care being influenced by a perceived do-or-die cultural standard they believe controls a business paradigm.

The Nelson team found that synthesizing both paradigms, however, can be effective at strengthening both closely held cultures. They suggest that corporate and business partnerships with schools are influencing school design principles while averting conflict. They offer three examples: the Business Roundtable, the Council for Corporate and School Partnerships, and the Boston Compact.

The Business Roundtable is an organization comprised of CEOs of some two hundred prominent U.S. corporations employing somewhere around thirty-four million people, who support various school reform activities, forums, and study implementations of the No Child Left Behind (2001) legislation. They focus on wide areas of diverse developmental issues such as academic instructional improvement, career awareness, civic and character education, drug abuse prevention, dropout prevention, and programs for the disadvantaged.

The Council for Corporate and School Partnerships supports and rewards schools engaged in partnership activities, while the Boston Compact has established a partnership between Boston's schools and the Boston Private Industry Council. Businesses promised students jobs if the schools were able to raise test scores and decrease dropout rates.

The Compact reports that businesses frequently come into the schools to teach, interact with students, and help teachers and counselors develop programs to improve student skills and attitudes. Partnerships have established work-study arrangements for students, produced teaching materials, and provided financial support for all aspects of schooling from teacher seminars to improving school technology and career guidance.

SUMMARY

Schools have a responsibility to provide the same opportunities for continuation students as they do comprehensive students. The cultural conflict, however, dividing those responsible for students living under adverse conditions confuses teachers who don't understand why their kids don't want to learn what they want to teach them. As such, resilient continuation students who, for the most part, ignore academic learning in favor of seeking credits that lead to their graduations, most often see continuation diplomas as less valuable.

Real-world success requires understanding that for every action, there is a reaction, a basic tenet of attribution theory. Continuation schools can no longer attempt to *benefit* its students by watering down its coursework or graduation requirements, two actions resulting in one devastating reaction.

"Unlike educational paradigms, corporations have made remarkable progress in building efficiency and productive gains. . . . Private enterprise cannot survive stagnation and as such, U.S. industries have avoided growth stoppage. . . . Improved technology and productivity could increase school efficiency considerably," say Nelson, Palonsky, and McCarthy (2007).

A generational conflict continues, however, between attitudes held by both education and business paradigms. Informal discussions with practitioners representing both concerns suggest that business personnel most often see themselves as incapable of dealing with educational challenges, and teachers do not want those in their care being influenced by a perceived do-or-die cultural standard they believe controls a business paradigm. The Business Roundtable, the Council for Corporate and School Partnerships, and the Boston Compact all demonstrate effective means of overcoming these concerns.

Chapter Three

Trust: A Strengths-Based Asset

Linkage research is described as an attempt at understanding questions behind a study's question (Tzafrir & Gur, 2007). It can be used to recognize organizational practices that are the most important drivers of student learning growth in a healthy continuation school, including, but not limited to, the construct of trust. Schneider and Bowen (1995), along with Schneider, White, and Paul (1998), offer glances at continuation school trust-building opportunities through linkage research applications.

As nurturing relationships build trust among stakeholders, significant improvement in studentwide learning occurs. Students in trusting, supportive educational environments advance rigor levels found in learning opportunities, rather than through course-directed requirements. Schneider's (1998) cohort found that when students trust caring and enthusiastic teachers, efforts provided by their schoolwide experiences most often reflect those very relationships.

Trust takes the form of *academic optimism*, a crucial characteristic of student learning. It builds upon the resources of a school's environmental and family communities. Trust building offers teachers and families opportunities at motivating student achievement through meaningful and relevant educational programming. A trust-centered building block can even go so far as to promote a safety net necessary to protect continuation schools from a culture of physical violence:

> Through daily vigilance, consistent consequences, and continual monitoring of progress with frequent midcourse corrections by adults, [trust-centered] schools wage war on low-level incivility. Leaders of these schools report that the school did not become truly safe until the students trusted that destructive behaviors would not be tolerated. Only then did they feel comfortable enough to trust each other. Once kids let the others know that we don't do that stuff in

our school, it all began to change. Kids took responsibility for their school and liked the way that felt. (Parrett & Budge, 2012, p. 114)

Trust-centered schools provide mutual respect between and among students and adults, providing a comfort zone that builds upon a rigorous and relevant schoolwide cultural foundation.

TRUSTING ADULT STAKEHOLDERS

The neglect and abuse suffered by a large percentage of our vulnerable highschoolers creates distrust. Bamburg (1994) teaches that an effective means of overcoming distrust begins with practitioners first building trust among and between themselves. A schoolwide faculty working together and trusting one another provides support for those who struggle with believing in others.

Bamburg believes in the value of faculty interactive collegiality as a trustbuilding mechanism. He tells us, "Changing expectations requires teachers to talk about their beliefs, assumptions, and practices. The kinds of communication needed must take place in an atmosphere of *collegiality* rather than *congeniality*" (in Dean & Parsley, 2011). He characterizes faculty collegiality by first identifying, then adopting, four teacher practices:

- talking a lot about practice
- observing one another teaching
- building curriculum together through planning, designing, researching, and evaluating
- learning from one another about teaching, learning, and leading (p. 3)

Mr. Ramos spent little to no time watching his colleague and friend, Ms. Littlefield, teach her art class. He focused instead on her students. He watched them squint their eyes as they concentrated on the model, tilting their heads back and forth, then holding up their pencils against her image with their fingers moving up and down to establish a proportion center, then its relationship to various other proportions found in various parts of the model's stance.

They studied her closely, before sketching her image on expensive paper taped to their drawing boards. They looked, positioned their drawing boards, looked again, sketched, erased, sketched, erased, and looked again, over and over. Higher-skilled students without prompt helped others at their table. The bell pushed students to get up, put their drawing boards away, and struggle off to their next classes. They appeared weary. They'd worked hard and were tired. Most importantly, their work showed they learned.

Ms. Littlefield told Mr. Ramos that in approximately three days, the class would pin their work on the easterly wall after placing their names on the backs of their drawings. The next class would then assess the qualities of each work based upon a set of standards, coupled with the value each piece brought to its purpose.

Mr. Ramos lit up.

Might it be possible to replicate this level of student concentration in his English/Language Arts classes? Could English students not only assess one another's work but also realize its value as clearly as Ms. Littlefield's art students did? Mr. Ramos went to work.

He began by having students flip through literary pieces found lying around each of their tables. Students shoved their personally chosen selections into the center of their tables before arguing the merits of their choices. Once each table agreed on a single selection, its members glanced at the board to select a common core standard that would give them their table's assignment. Again, all needed to agree on the selected standard. Each table elected a group leader who recorded student-selected activities that would build upon the standard's requirements.

Classroom noise levels increased as small groups of students waved at each other before grabbing one another's arms trying to get their attention. They looked at each other intently, positioning their points back and forth, trying to get others to agree. Once accomplished, students used the same process back and forth, trying to build their paper's positions. They yelled their position, backed off when they liked another's better, yelled their position, got excited when others agreed, yelled another position point, taking notes and arguing positions. Back and forth.

When their projects were complete, another class heard each table's presentation, studied copies of their papers, then assessed the qualities of each work based upon a concrete set of standards, coupled with the value each paper brought to its purpose.

The bell pushed students from their seats. They put their note-filled folders away and struggled off to their next classes. They looked weary. They'd worked hard and were tired. Most importantly, their work showed they learned.

***

Krovetz and Arriaza (2006) further Bamburg's perspective when discussing a depth level trusting adults can bring to any school, continuation, or comprehensive. The researchers suggest that a school's overall levels of optimism and pessimism influence a teacher's thought habits, as both strongly affect schoolwide trust. And when a school is processing change, leaders must be intentional about the way they interpret and communicate setbacks as their interpretations will affect how site-level stakeholders view these events, thereby once again affecting schoolwide trust.

Interviewed dropouts report that in order to build the trust of struggling students, faculties must listen; listen, that is, to their students' views, experiences, concerns, life circumstances, and various reform ideas (Bridgeland, Dilulio, & Burke-Morison, 2006). They argue that those providing resources must use them to create smaller classes with more one-on-one instruction, involvement, and feedback.

Bridgeland posits that decision makers should attract better teachers who might not only keep classes interesting but also somehow make the lessons more relevant and engaging as they build upon a connection between school and work.

***

"I dunno. Mr. Ramos, I guess," replied Merari to Kristi's question. "All of us had favorite teachers when we were kids; you know, like Ms. Adams in the second grade. Everyone loved her. I loved it when she put me on her lap and taught me how to tie my shoes." Merari continued, "Yea, remember when she sat with you and like, made you feel really cared for . . . almost like your mom?"

"I learned so much from her," said Kristi. "Even though it was only the second grade, we all knew our times tables and were working on division problems by the end of the year. And we loved it! Remember? Ms. Adams was great. You think Mr. Ramos is like that?"

"Well yea, but different. You know? It's like, teachers who got it together care about you and make you learn a lot," said Merari. "How do you find teachers like that?"

"You know," Kristi answered, "sometimes I think you can. Sometimes, I think if you could identify the exact traits of a great teacher . . . "

"Yea," Merari said. "And those traits could compare to those of a great mom."

"Okay," interrupted Kristi, "and she was the kinda mom who really made you wanna do well at absolutely everything, you know? The kinda mom who got as excited as you do, and . . . "

"Yea, Yea!" Merari chimed in. "Okay. Now one side of her would have your back and the other side showed how important your school work is to your life . . . know what I mean?"

"Yeaaaa," sighed Merari. "But where would you find a teacher like that?"

With a slow exhale, Kristi commented with, "Dunno. Heard somewhere that Mr. Ramos used to teach kindergarten . . . "

"Yea, I heard that too. You think high schools should ask kindergarten teachers to teach us?"

"Naaaw, that's crazy. But you know, maybe kindergarten teachers could help high school teachers teach a lot better."

Gardner (1993) discusses instructional concepts aligned with multiple intelligences that can lead to trust strengthening among and between all educational change stakeholders, including students and faculty as well as both site and district leaders. He may well be suggesting that various stakeholder intelligences, working with students failing to meet schoolwide normative standards, are actually potentials for developing personally successful, satisfying strategies that meet academic challenges.

Strengthening trust among stakeholders may very well allow Gardner's thoughts to employ critical literacy as a means of using basic school knowledge to identify and correct significant power disparities between haves and have-nots (Friere, 1970; Friere & Macedo, 1987; Comber & Simpson, 2001).

Friere involves the development of critical consciousness, using communication to expose oppression. Teacher and student are co-intentional, sharing equally in dialogues on social reality and developing critical understandings that can liberate them from the culture of silence. Thus, the term *literate* may be thought of as a verbal badge given to those who possess knowledge considered socially valuable (Nelson, Palonsky, & McCarthy, 2007, p. 236).

TRUSTING CHOICE

Classroom observations, alongside faculty room discussions, indicate that coercive curriculum and instruction dominate schoolwide curriculums and classroom strategies. It is thought that practitioners most often view *student choice* as destructive to student growth. They contend that students simply do not know what they need to know, thereby requiring practitioners to tell them.

Practitioners, according to practitioners, need and deserve to be trusted to tell students what they need to know and specifically what they need to do to learn it. Students who please practitioners are considered successful, while those who do not are often described as lazy.

This collection of beliefs finds itself at the center of continuation school program design and is a primary determiner for blocking student growth. Evidence shows that student choice not only builds upon student self-efficacy, a feature of learning motivation leading to achievement, it also begins the defeat of student vulnerability. Senses of self-efficacy erect powerful self-images within and among our most resilient student strugglers (Seligman, 1990; Noddings, 2003; Kirby & DiPaola, 2009; Boykin & Noguera, 2011).

***

Successful students graduate, and graduates become teachers. If, as often discussed, teachers teach as they were taught, then it's fitting that teachers resist change, that they cling to their perceived classroom control rather than losing it to student choice. This resistance avoids the term *responsibility*, which if paired with *choice*, sheds a fresh, new light upon classroom engagement and learning effectiveness.

***

Subject matter exposure, as Noddings (2003) describes it, "is a form of coercion but, without the usual competitive grading." It employs the term *responsible choice*. It depends heavily upon informal learning. It allows and supports topical study instead of demanding it. "Why, for example, do we offer poetry?" she asks. "If our answer is that poetry may become a lifelong source of delight and wisdom, then it must be offered as a source of happiness *now*." She continues:

> Many children would have no idea that their interests might be intellectual if the school does nothing to introduce them to the life of the mind. But the purpose of opening doors is to invite children to explore so that they can find out how these new ideas fit their own purposes. (pp. 207–8)

It can be argued that teachers *introducing*, *offering*, *exploring*, and *opening doors* induce student choice rather than gentle coercion. Trusting begets learning. Students who trust model the behaviors of those they trust—their teachers. They ask their teachers what's important to learn and why. They reach out in all learning arenas, then choose to learn what they need to know to achieve what they wish to achieve. Thinkers need not justify their persuasions or beliefs, but rather to simply trust choice.

Practitioners creating rigorous educational programs, relevant to student wants and needs and infused with a standards-based learning foundation, produce effective results in paradigms outside education. Changers and practitioners would do well to investigate student growth that can be brought about by student curiosity and advanced through choice.

***

Coercion is a common continuation school strategic failure, a decoupled element inherited from a district's comprehensive classroom culture. Practitioners ask how *student choice* might be different. Student achievement found within a culture of choice initiates a schoolwide trust, trust not only in student capacity but in stakeholder interactions as well. "What things really matter?" asks Noddings (2003):

> Every topic, attribute, or skill that contributes to human flourishing matters educationally and the most important things for schools to treat are those that

provide a foundation for further learning and growing. Howard Gardner emphasizes that multiple intelligences are used as pedagogical hooks to help students learn the standard subjects. I prefer to develop them for their own sake, cherishing each as an end in itself and also as a stepping stone for children who find their talents in one area or another. (p. 208)

Realizing a delicate balance between coercive tactics and pedagogical choice, Noddings suggests, "Students can be invited to read the novels of Hemingway, Steinbeck, and Faulkner. The books should not be chosen simply because they might be part of the academic curriculum, but because they fit the interests of vocational students and because they are thought by many of us to be fine works. Both quality and relevance are important" (p. 213).

Even though somewhat cautious, Noddings supports a meeting of challenging goals and high standards through student choice. Students tend to work at tough tasks primarily if they are connected to the end results. Within the required courses, however, she teaches that there needs to be room for enjoyment provided by student choice and optional exploration. Student choice embodies a pedagogical requirement for classroom change necessary for student learning—true learning.

"I would like students to be able to *try out* the study of mathematics, physics, the visual arts, great music, fine literature, and other subjects that have been forced on students in the past." She describes mini-courses being offered as "personal exploration to open avenues of possible study in the future and simply for enjoyment. Middle school years could be three glorious years of such risk-free exploration" (pp. 206–7).

Evaluation in these years should be formative, allowing for summative assessments to be administered at the end of middle school. The summative assessments can establish a curriculum formation in high school.

RESPECT: A FOUNDATIONAL ASSET

Respect rarely needs to be defined. Students in their own ways see it as a positive view held of another, an evaluated belief that something or someone is important, held in high esteem, and well received by others. Respect offers a powerful feeling of admiration and acceptance, aimed at another's beliefs or behavior—most effective, it is argued, when first aimed at oneself. Students, for the most part, absolutely demand respect as a source of perceived power. Respect is a foundational attribute, supporting effective study, program development, and a healthy schoolwide culture.

Respect is a feeling that drives behavior. When students learn that their teacher cares about them, supports them, and expects from them, a rush of warmth drives students to defend their teachers against all manners of criticism and threat, behaviors that reflect *respect*. As teachers believe and trust that their programs support student learning, they take ownership of their programs, a behavior that also drives *respect*. And schools, no matter what, must defend their students. *Respect* demands it.

***

Franklin knew he wasn't respected. Truth is, he didn't know what *respect* was. He spent his short sixteen years avoiding others. He had no friends and only a remnant of a family that ignored him. He lived in an apathetic state of existence. He knew no other—no other, that is, until a young, freshly ordained pastor discovered him digging through waste cans and offered him breakfast.

It wasn't so much the idea of *respect* that the minister offered him. It was a strong, caring concern extended by the young pastor and built upon a faith that Franklin had never before realized. And the intensity of the pastor's faith provided a love that Franklin had also never felt. He was lost and confused. The fresh, new, exciting feeling was scary. Franklin couldn't shake it, and at the same time, wouldn't allow himself to believe it. He kept imagining how he would handle losing it someday, a thought that terrified him.

The young pastor and Franklin gradually established a bonding friendship, built upon a foundation of trust, a trust so strong that Franklin believed it infinitely perpetual, so enduring that it erased his fear of loss. The relationship, for the first time, exposed a feeling of *respect*, one that Franklin would later describe as "a feeling only possible through a personal relationship with my Lord and Savior, Jesus Christ." And, upon enrolling at his district's continuation high school, Franklin aggressively preached his message to his teachers, staff, and fellow students wherever and whenever opportunity presented itself.

Franklin found himself no longer ignored.

As might be expected, students and staff avoided Franklin and his preaching, a relational tactic known only too well by Franklin. Franklin preached anyway. Students jeered and scoffed at him, grinning behind his back. Teachers encouraged him to adopt respectful behaviors accepted by his peers. Franklin preached anyway. Then something happened. A young, attractive female student, one well respected by the others, asked Franklin about his beliefs. He offered her breakfast.

ASSETS AND OUTCOMES: STUDENT GROWTH DEVELOPMENT

He simply wanted others to feel the way he felt. The results of Franklin's behavior fortified his beliefs, however his intentions. Motivation is not always related to meaning. Purpose is not a factor in the basic tenets offered by

Ellis and Harper's pedagogical framework (1997). Franklin's results, however, elaborate upon his feelings, which strengthen his behavior. Schoolwide efforts offer similar growth opportunities as, like in Franklin's case, seen through behavioral outcomes.

Learning occurs when it's sought out, when it's wanted. Relevant motivation appears in many formats while irrelevant learning manifests itself often in academic testing. Performance-based assessments demonstrate the proud achievements of one who has accomplished. No one demonstrates a failed outcome. Only tests are failed. Learning criteria must be chosen as well as its methodologies, formative assessments, and summative performances.

***

A student sees a beautiful, well-engineered cutting block produced by a former student in his shop class. He wants to make one. Another is spellbound by the harmonies provided by a piece of music performed by her school orchestra. She imagines warm feelings rushing through her as she joins them with her viola. A student watercolor, matted, framed, and hanging in the school office, evidences affective learning in three of the five basic elements of visual design. It hangs just above a student's matted and framed mathematical formula demonstrating a pricing technique for discounted retail products, including any local sales taxes.

The school hallways are lined with student essay samples arguing varying merits of historic U.S. Supreme Court decisions requiring a thorough understanding of five English/Language Arts common core standards. A group of students discovered unique DNA molecular structures found in local pine needle oils that may well upset human health theories published in state-adopted biology texts. They formally presented their concerns to a small group of biology instructors from their local community college. Members of the district school board, along with the superintendent's staff, were also in attendance.

SUMMARY

Caring is essential. When students trust caring teachers, perceptions of their school experiences reflect those relationships. Trust leads to academic optimism, a characteristic enhancing student learning. Trust offers opportunities at motivating student achievement, promoting safety nets that protect against all challenges, including physical violence. It builds mutual respect between students and teachers while creating a rigorous, high-level academic environment.

Trust building requires adults to re-think their listening habits involving student viewpoints, experiences, and life circumstances. It challenges adults to listen to their various reform ideas. Schools must trust resource providers to create smaller classes, more one-on-one instruction, student/teacher involvement, and feedback.

Student choice is a powerful academic protective factor, protecting against threatening acts of failure propagated by decoupled continuation school design. It builds upon student self-efficacy, which defeats student vulnerability. *Responsibility* paired with *choice* strengthens classroom engagement and learning effectiveness while strengthening trust. Trust begets learning.

Respect, yet another strong protective factor, offers a powerful feeling of admiration and acceptance aimed at another's beliefs or behavior; yet it is most effective when one trusts oneself. It's the foundation of learning that takes the form of relevancy when assessed in a performance setting. No one performs a failed outcome. Only tests are failed.

Chapter Four

Generating College and Career Readiness

On August 2, 2010, thirty-four states and the District of Columbia adopted what is now referred to as the Common Core State Standards Initiative (CCSS) for the purpose of standardizing student achievement levels in English/Language Arts and mathematics. The Standards were designed to provide clear understandings of what students are expected to learn as demonstrated by knowledge and skill-level achievement indicators necessary for college and career readiness.

Attention is given to reading/writing standards in history/social studies, science, and technical subjects, integrated in meaningful ways to help students acquire high levels of academic capabilities that promote student successes in higher-level coursework and career-level job placement. The Council of Chief State School Officers (CCSSO) and the National Governors Association (NGA) suggest that the newly adopted Common Core Standards meet or exceed these requirements.

IDENTIFYING COLLEGE AND CAREER REQUIREMENT INDICATORS

While generally accepted that college entrance demands align with standardized student capabilities, career requirements often entail another look, one extending additional specificity. Academically, a student may be asked to cite strong and thorough textual evidence to support an analysis, whereas professionally, she may need to identify two or more central ideas of a product's benefits to determine its strength in a marketplace. It's noteworthy, however, to realize that in both cases, standardized efforts serve both study and professional needs.

***

Employers at all levels agree that educating and training new hires is their responsibility, one they do not wish to pass on to schools. Basic knowledge and skill levels, however, are fundamental to supporting employer efforts.

Information is readily available, laying out the tenets of the CCSS Initiative. Of primary concern, however, is a student's ability to integrate into the culture of those providing opportunities. The Initiative attempts to satisfy this concern, accordingly:

> To build a foundation for college and career readiness, students must have ample opportunities to take part in a variety of rich, structured conversations—as part of a whole class, in small groups, and with a partner. Being productive members of these conversations requires that students contribute accurate, relevant information; respond to and develop what others have said; make comparisons and contrasts; and analyze and synthesize a multitude of ideas in various domains. (http://www.corestandards.org)

SYNTHESIZING INDICATORS WITH COMMON CORE STANDARDS

Faculty room conversations often conclude that colleges provide academics, while careers, for the most part, deliver economical outcomes. Some suggest that schools teach thought while professions profit from those thoughts. Asking professionals to provide academics (or to teach thought) is like asking teachers to produce economical outcomes or to profit from thought.

College and career readiness, therefore, offer two opposing notions: thought and profit. The two concepts lack relationship. Teachers are ill prepared to synthesize career readiness requirements with common core standards, and as such, are predicted to push what they know, academics. They will avoid any hint of career readiness lessoning, an inimical consequence for all students, alternative and otherwise.

The Initiative's description assumes that schools and K–12 teachers are qualified to not only provide these *ample opportunities* but also to guide student growth in a professional, career-readiness manner. In a continuation setting, however, students often contribute to the economic health and stability of their families. One way to satisfy their career readiness concerns through a CCSS amplified relevancy, some say, is to establish an on-campus career center that provides career-oriented job opportunities for students and their families.

Rich, structured conversational criteria incorporating what others in career settings commonly use can be identified through actual student and family experiences, applied to schoolwide lesson designs, and integrated among and within staff, student, and stakeholder discussions.

***

Academically, Common Core Literacy Standards for Writing in History/Social Studies 6-12 (2a) says to write informative/explanatory texts to examine and convey complex ideas, concepts, and information clearly and accurately through the effective selection, organization, and analysis of content; while Speaking and Listening Standards 6-12 (4) says to present information, findings, and supporting evidence conveying a clear and distinct perspective such that listeners can follow the line of reasoning.

As a *career readiness* lesson exposes a student-manager opportunity, standards might adjust to read: Writing 6-12: 2a. Include as part of a personal resume an informative/explanatory proposal that allocates firsthand evidence examining information, concepts, and complex ideas supplied by former as well as current employees that clearly and accurately provide criteria that can significantly reduce existing high levels of employee turnover; and Speaking and Listening 6-12: 4. Present information, findings, and supporting evidence conveying a clear and distinct solution to a company's turnover problem such that employers can follow the line of reasoning.

ASSESSING GROWTH

Educational assessments, for the most part, simply ask, What does one want to know, and how can that knowledge lead to improved learning? Assessing growth, occurring through actual student learning provided by the 6-12 Writing, Listening and Speaking standards, appears in continuation schools in very unexpected ways, both academically and professionally. The following represent both an academic and career-oriented assessment at mastering a Writing 6-12 (2) attempt:

A student felt an author's moment while scanning the look on Scout's face. Scout simply said, "Hey, Boo . . . "

The student immediately selected this moment in Harper Lee's *To Kill a Mockingbird* to write an examination of the moment in support of the book's message, by conveying Lee's ideas and concepts clearly through analysis of the content. She simplified an outline of Lee's complex ideas exposed in Scout's welcoming comment to better understand an earlier experience of her own. Her essay would be numbered for anonymity, and read by students from another class who would base their assessments on schoolwide supported rubric criteria.

She used her paper to defend thoughts and feelings inherent in her own experience.

***

Its reputation preceded it. It paid more, offered flexible hours, and employed young, career-oriented twenty-year-olds in management positions. It was the hottest job in town, so Franklin needed a fresh, attention-getting approach, one he found in his school standard, Writing 6-12: 2a.

He contacted fast food managers throughout his community, asking for evidence-gathering interviews. He told them he was doing an employer-employee study exposing the most pressing concerns of each participant group. He wanted to know what was being done about employer concerns as well as any results transpiring from both employer and employee decisions. As compensation, Franklin would, of course, provide each participant with the results of the study.

Once he had examined the analyses and conclusions befalling the study's interview data, Franklin contacted the general manager of *the hottest job in town*. He presented her with not only his findings but conclusions and recommendations provided by her local competitors as well. He presented informative findings that examined and conveyed complex information clearly and accurately through an effective analysis of its content.

One interviewer offered Franklin a line cook position on the spot. Two other managers contacted him the following day with job offers as well. *The hottest job in town*, however, was in the market for career-oriented managers, and they were hard to find. Franklin reported for his first managerial training session a week and a half later.

***

It was like trying to recall a rock thrown at a window. Once she became unconscious, the abortion procedure would follow its path to fruition. Her fear caused confusion that oppressed her senses, all because she was trying to impress a couple of so-called friends.

Student social activities in Serena's continuation high school exposed an overwhelming need for students to realize the many outcomes of consequential behaviors. The desire for external respect is significant among high school students, and Serena removed hers through self-reflection, an activity leading her to study the three consequences of teen pregnancy. She wanted to present her findings to those hiding from their consequential conduct.

She used her Common Core Standard, Speaking and Listening 6-12 (4) to present supporting evidence that would convey her clear and distinct perspective, allowing her audience to follow her line of reasoning.

Standing behind a classroom podium provided by her third-period social studies teacher, Serena opened her presentation with, "I'm pregnant and I don't know what to do."

The class froze, eyes widened and mouths hung open. Dead silence.

Twenty-three pairs of eyes stared directly into hers as she threw up her hands and cried out, "It was no big deal, ya know? I mean, really!" Tears dripped from her chin. " My so-called friends told me everyone was doing it and the worst thing in the world was to be a virgin! Now what in the hell am I supposed to do? My parents don't even know."

She fumbled through some notes while trying to dry her face. "Okay. I'm going to share some evidence I dug up while preparing for this presentation. You guys won't believe how stupid we girls are . . . " and with that, Serena presented her information, findings, and supporting evidence. Upon conclusion, she asked for the advice and support of her fellow classmates. She received plenty of both.

Somewhere near a week and a half later, Serena fell upon a Langston Hughes essay offering a fresh look at life as a black man in twentieth-century America. She was stunned. She wondered what actions would be encouraged if she could present Hughes's points of view as effectively as her pregnancy effort.

***

"I am concerned about overall working conditions I observed from visiting restaurants and interviewing their general managers around town, Ma'am," Franklin opened with Mrs. Williams, the general manager of *the hottest job in town*. Looking for the effect of his attention-getter, Franklin continued with, " And the reputation preceding your restaurant, Ma'am, suggests that you folks have pretty much overcome those obstacles. May I have a few moments?"

As Franklin offered his hand, he quietly commented, "Thank you very much for seeing me, Mrs. Williams. I am Franklin Willower, a recent graduate from Sem Yeto High, and it seems that employee complacency and apathy have invaded our local restaurants."

"Oh?" she curiously responded while rating this young man.

Franklin spent no more than five minutes presenting his findings and supporting evidence, conveying a clear and distinct perspective held by former and current employees of local fast food restaurants. His line of reasoning fell in line with the significant number of concerns Mrs. Williams most recently had while staffing her brand new, fast food franchise. As Franklin's questions piggybacked other manager's concerns, he kept her interest by concluding each point with a question and adding beneficial comments to her answers.

Mrs. Williams responded by asking Franklin if he would entertain a further, more in-depth discussion at 10:30 a.m., the upcoming Wednesday. She mentioned needing to make a few phone calls first. As Franklin left her a copy of his professionally bound set of findings, he smiled, nodded, and let her know he looked forward to their upcoming meeting.

He grinned while mentally reviewing his presentation of information, findings, and supporting evidence that conveyed clear and distinct perspectives to his new boss.

***

Changers must ask themselves, Do continuation teachers for the most part believe their students capable of learning at CCSS levels? In what ways might this belief create feelings that drive curriculum design into either perpetuating or defeating existing continuation learning levels?

SUMMARY

In 2010, the Common Core State Standards Initiative (CCSS) was adopted by the District of Columbia and thirty-four states. Its purpose was to standardize student achievement levels in English and math. While the initiative works toward preparing students for college readiness, it fails to address any relationship those levels might have with a career readiness capacity. While college entrance demands align with standardized student capabilities, career requirements often entail another look, one extending additional specificity.

For example, academically, a student may be asked to cite strong and thorough textual evidence to support an analysis, whereas career-wise, she may need to identify two or more central ideas of a product's benefits to determine its strength in a marketplace. Employers at all levels agree that educating and training new hires is their responsibility, one they embrace and do not wish to pass on to schools. Basic knowledge and skill levels, however, are foundational to supporting employer efforts.

Colleges provide academics while careers most often allocate economic outcomes. Some suggest that schools teach thought while professionals profit from those thoughts. Asking professionals to provide academics (or to teach thought) is like asking teachers to produce economic outcomes or to profit from thought.

Teachers are ill prepared to synthesize career readiness growth with common core standards, and as such, will push what they know, academics. They will avoid any hint of career readiness lessoning. One possibility at satisfying their career readiness concerns through a CCSS-amplified relevancy is to establish an on-campus career center that provides career-oriented job opportunities for students and their families.

Rich, structured conversational criteria incorporating what others in career settings commonly say can be identified through actual student and family experiences, applied to schoolwide lesson designs, and integrated among and within staff, student, and stakeholder discussions alike.

II

Augmenting Formidable and Arduous Learning

Chapter Five

Strengthening School Design

Strengthening curriculum and instruction is rooted in a cultural attitude of "We, as a school can," a schoolwide sense of efficacy . . . an academic optimism if you will, seen through academic press. Student efficacy, appearing through academic press, offers a steadfast focus in which to build a healthy school design with the sole purpose of benefiting student growth and achievement.

***

Strong, healthy school and classroom design, found in strengths-based continuation schools, can be developed through targeted interventions that will enhance student engagement and lead to elevated levels of academic achievement (Schunk, 2003). Targeted interventions have been developed that link key information to Schunk's tenet:

- produce evidence over a longitudinal history of successful academic performances and experiences
- allow stakeholders to:

  - use their observations of student learning to improve program design and development
  - use verbal persuasion and/or social influences to encourage all students to achieve at high levels
  - develop schoolwide environments filled with feelings of relaxation, confidence, and happiness. (Bandura, 1994, in Nelson, Palonsky, & McCarthy, 2007, pp. 150–51)

Concerned with findings from the Coleman Report (1966) saying that student socioeconomical status (SES) determined student academic achievement, Kirby and DiPaola (2009) looked at conclusions reached by Brookover and Lezotte (1979), Edmonds (1979, 1981), and Hallinger and Murphy (1986), suggesting that *academic optimism* is at the root of all successful schoolwide achievement. It possesses characteristics such as strong instructional leadership, a pervasive emphasis on academics, high student expectations, and a safe and orderly learning environment.

Other studies added characteristics that include open, healthy school climates, collegial principal leadership, professional teacher behaviors, academic press, and community engagement (DiPaola & Tschannen-Moran, 2005; Erbe, 2000; Hoy & Hannum, 1997; Hoy, Hannum, & Tschannen-Moran, 1998; Lee, Smith, Perry, & Smylie, 1999; Paredes, 1991; Zigarelli, 1996).

***

Kirby and DiPaola (2009), while looking for student achievement assets, uncovered relationships between *academic optimism* and *school climate*, both influencing student achievement despite Coleman's SES limitations. They looked at three traits representing cognitive, affective, and behavioral aspects of academic optimism: collective efficacy, trust in students and parents, and academic press, all strength-building school-design components. They found that:

- collective teacher efficacy, the extent to which teachers as a faculty can cause a particular outcome, must rely upon a faculty-held belief that positive teacher influences help students make choices that will enhance their achievements
- trust, as an affective aspect of academic optimism, must prevail as a crucial characteristic found to enhance learning
- academic press results from a school's focus on academics
- the following schoolwide characteristics must be intact:
  - significant schoolwide efforts
  - recognized achievements
  - teachers acting in ways that reflect their beliefs that students can be motivated to work hard and meet high expectations. (Bryk, Lee, & Holland, 1993; Goddard, Hoy, & Woolfolk-Hoy, 2004; Hoy, Tarter, & Woolfolk-Hoy, 2007)

Boykin and Noguera's (2011) work discusses the effects of an effective school design upon self-improvement. Self-improvement is not only under one's control, it may well be linked to the application of effort, persistence, and learning across time, and attitudinal conditions of one's academic capacities—his or her intelligence, if you will. There is compelling evidence that what a student thinks about his or her intelligence can have a powerful effect on his or her achievement (Aronson, Fried, and Good, 2002).

***

Students often discuss social and family interactions that expose stubborn attitudes held by others as selfish, opinionated, and/or pigheaded, traits identified as *fixed views*. Fixed views tend to be more centered on preserving self-respect than with trying to improve performance on a particular task. Students with malleable views, on the other hand, likely see failure as an opportunity to get better at a skill. They most often profit from their mistakes, causing them to improve their efforts:

> In the face of failure, entity-focused students are more inclined to compare themselves with lower-achievers. It's as if they seek to verify that they see themselves as somehow capable. Incremental-focused students, on the other hand, try to determine which strategies are used by higher-achieving classmates as they hope to improve their own performances. (Boykin & Noguera, 2011, p. 63)

A question arises as to whether fixed rather than malleable views of intelligence are open to change. Evidence discussed by Mueller and Dweck (1998) suggest that fixed views can convert to malleable views at perhaps relatively young ages.

Good, Aronson, and Inzlicht (2003) studied a sample of low-income, racially diverse seventh-graders who were mentored by college students who provided them with school adjustment and study strategies while encouraging them to regard intelligence as malleable. The study group compared their *experimental* group with a seventh-grade control group deprived of information regarding intelligence and reasons for academic difficulties.

The results showed that girls in the experimental group performed substantially better than their peers in the control group. Boys in both groups had essentially the same math performance levels with a slight increase by boys in the experimental group. Reading scores remained stable across gender for condition, strengthening findings that students in the experimental group performed better than students in the control group.

Good's study group learned that students who were praised for their abilities rather than their efforts on a basic, elementary set of matrix problems had less desire to persist with more difficult problems, expressed less task enjoyment, and performed more poorly after experiencing a period of failure (in Boykin & Noguera, 2011, pp. 66–67).

Further study of conceptual and empirical links between malleable views of intelligence, self-efficacy, and self-regulation can be found in the works of Aronson, Fried, and Good (2002), Bandura (1994), Chan and Moore (2006), Dweck (1999), Linnenbrink and Pintrich (2003), Lynch (2008), Molden and Dweck (2006), Seifert (2004), and Shell and Husman (2008).

DEVELOPING PROGRAM DESIGN

Evidence strongly suggests that alternative school program design needs an ethnographic platform that strengthens and defines a school's purpose. Although program designers understand that purpose varies, Nelson, Palonsky, and McCarthy (2007) argue that examining, conveying, questioning, and modifying knowledge are the building blocks of school purpose. And that responsibility, according to Nelson's cohort, should frame a school's pedagogy.

A unique curriculum design, reported by Liana Heitin in her article for *Education Week* (April 18, 2012) titled "Flattening the School Walls," discusses Tom Horn's effectiveness with his alternative education program in Cottage Grove, Oregon. Heitin's report exemplifies a school that replaced an internally struggling academic program with an external, project-based design to replace academics with a *real-world* pedagogical model.

Horn, an alternative school principal, determined that his school needed a *student-engaging* curriculum, one that strengthens student mind-sets. He chose a project-based learning model with a theme of *sustainability*. He divided students into five groups with each completing projects related to a subtheme of one of the topics of agriculture, energy, forestry, architecture, or water.

Students remained with the same teacher all day so that each teacher could extend, end, or come back to a lesson the next day, whatever became necessary to meet student achievement goals. With a five-member faculty, four instructional aides, and around sixty community volunteers who helped and supported with various projects, the principal assembled his [continuation] high school team.

Horn describes project-based learning as:

> working down Bloom's taxonomy instead of up. Students are given a task that requires higher-order thinking skills—often to create something—requiring them to learn and practice lower-level skills along the way. The standards are embedded into the projects from the start. Horn and his staff map out each project on a matrix, with the content subjects on the horizontal and phases of the project on the vertical. The standards are embedded into the boxes. (Heitin, 2012, pp. 5–6)

Students follow up with a battery of formative assessments throughout the year to determine the status of their basic skills levels. Teachers allow time for individual interventions based upon those results. Every student has an individualized plan.

Horn's program ignited student attentiveness, relevance, and resonance as evidenced by an overall upsurge in student attendance and engagement.

Test scores, however, struggled.

Heitin reports that as of 2012, Horn's school is behind the state average passing rate on all three Oregon state academic assessments: reading, writing, and math. While reading scores have significantly increased from 9 to 52 percent and math scores have improved from 18 to 36 percent, Heitin reports that writing assessments "bounce around creating an inconsistent set of scores."

Schools, according to Nelson, Palonsky, and McCarthy (2007), should "give more importance not just to reading but to basic skills and workplace values . . . to improve instruction in the knowledge and attitudes that contribute to our society and to provide education that reflects the society" (p. 208).

ROADBLOCKS AND CHALLENGES

Continuation school design most often competes with social forces, with social forces prevailing. Its curriculum is commonly watered-down and apathetically approached by school boards, district- and site-level leadership, and most concerning, teachers themselves. States see continuation schools as graduation resources, nothing more and nothing less. Teacher-held attitudes about the adverse conditions of alternative students control not only what should be taught, but at what levels.

School-led teacher interactions are mostly about fear—fear of losing control. "Every year, our schools are becoming bigger and bigger catch basins of unfinished family of origin business; catch basins influencing every person in them" (Dallmann-Jones, 2006, p. 88). Dysfunctionality becomes a denial. He calls this a definition for a *highly toxic environment*.

School curriculum also adds to the controversy. While stakeholders are asking if all students should or need to take the same courses, effective and meaningful school re-framing requires educational decision makers to think more about what should be taught and why. It demands that they consider what is to be learned and how. If the value of a lesson is not clearly visible or lacks student want, as often seen with required courses, extraneous benefits such as student gifts, happy lesson activities, and optional student exploration come into play.

Why not simply demonstrate the value of the lesson?

***

It's a shame that vocational programs, rich in relevancy, take a rear seat to academics—aka intellectual material—seen as irrelevant to practicality. Vocational programs prepare students for jobs while academics equip them for higher education, which in turn assumes higher-paying jobs. Yet so often, when academics support the few who embrace it, its irrelevancy punishes those who do not. Academic strugglers are typically assigned to technical programs such as shop, home economics, or crafts because they weren't deemed *good enough* to handle the preferred academic program.

Charles W. Eliot, president of Harvard University who argued strongly for an academic curriculum for all, rather than one geared to *probable destinies*, said, "Too often, vocational programs have been *enriched* by simply adding on or plugging in material from the academic curriculum. This is sometimes called integrating academic and vocational studies. But the vocational program should serve as a screen or lens for the choice of rich intellectual material" (in Noddings, 2003, p. 210).

***

Wang, Haertel, and Walberg (1994) favor a replacement of existing educational design contradictions with renewed emphasis on psychological, instructional, and contextual influences:

> Fifty years of research contradict educators' current reliance on school restructuring and organizational variables as key components of school reform. Because indirect influences may only affect direct influences, they appear to be weaker and less consistent in their results. Changing policies is unlikely to change practices in classrooms and homes, where learning actually takes place. Better alignment of remote policies and direct practices and more direct intervention in the psychological determinants of learning promise the most effective avenues of reform. (p. 79)

QUESTIONING DESIGN

Questioning design must address educational designs that go beyond simply improving test scores. Noddings (2003) asks if program design, for example, should develop understanding and prevent violence rather than simply improving mathematical and scientific literacy.

- Should we offer courses in peace education, understanding and treating substance abuse, along with promoting self-understanding and interpersonal relations?

- What about protecting the environment, teaching love of place, parenting, spiritual awakening, and preparing for a congenial occupation?
- Rather than grading students for their abilities (or lack thereof) in identifying famous works of art, might we encourage lasting pleasure in all arts and develop sound characters and pleasing personalities? (p. 200)

Do designs built upon these and other analogous questions bring about college and career readiness for our most vulnerable high-schoolers? Are they designed to? Are they more important concerns than those built upon high-reaching, elevated academic designs? Program designers may well ask, What do those implementing the programs want for their own kids?

***

Questioning school program design invokes once again a questioning of student choice. Student choice exposes student *wants*, which when identified as *defined wants*, can measure academic motivators. Measuring academic motivators generates empirical evidence leading to findings beneficial to student growth. Looking at student *wants* for the purpose of building educational program design offers the following beliefs:

- Unlike impulsive urges, *wants* are fairly stable over a considerable period of time.
- *Wants* are demonstrably connected to some desirable end or, at least, to one that is not harmful . . . the end is impossible or difficult to reach without the object wanted.
- *Wants* are in the power and within the means of those asked to grant them.
- The person *wanting* is willing and able to contribute to the satisfaction of the want. (Noddings, 2003, p. 61)

Educators who take seriously the ideas and intuitions of their students are more likely to achieve success than those ignoring their views, suggests Gardner (2011). Children's ideas, for the most part, remain throughout their lives. He teaches that their ideas must first be taken seriously so they may truly understand what they learn. It's another way of saying their learning becomes a part of them.

CONNECTEDNESS: A STRENGTH-BASED PROTECTIVE FACTOR

The Centers for Disease Control and Prevention (CDC) offers a workable description for the term *protective factors* in their 2007 *Adolescent and School Health* article, "Protective Factors and School Connectedness":

> Protective factors are individual or environmental characteristics, conditions, or behaviors that reduce the effects of stressful life events. These factors also increase an individual's ability to avoid risks or hazards, and promote social and emotional competence to thrive in all aspects of life, now and in the future.
>
> School connectedness —the belief held by students that adults and peers in the school care about their learning as well as about them as individuals—is an important protective factor. Research has shown that young people who feel connected to their school are less likely to engage in many risk behaviors, including early sexual initiation, alcohol, tobacco, and other drug use, and violence and gang involvement. Students who feel connected to their school are also more likely to have better academic achievement, including higher grades and test scores, have better school attendance, and stay in school longer. (p. 1)

Connectedness grows from a school design that employs parents at all engagement levels. Evidence shows that involving family members in school activities frequently demonstrates parents attending college along with employment-related workshops. Parents also volunteer with school activities, working with their child on homework and discussing school more often. Discussions involving familial cultural and class differences honor student diversities, and, more often than not, further engage members of the community.

Communication is sorely lacking between continuation schools and parents. Schools need to strengthen connectedness by reaching out to parents, asking them to share in and be a part of the school's solutions. Parents need to know and understand the value of their input in continuation education. As parent apathy toward their children's schooling often shows up in truancy, frequent teacher/parent communications are necessary to keep kids in school, say interviewed dropouts.

Schools would profit from addressing different types of family circumstances, thereby shrinking school-family differences such as language, culture, and educational attainment or simply reaching a single working parent. Developing individualized graduation plans together with parents and school personnel directly supports a continuation student's motivation to graduate. It allows parents and students a stronger awareness of not only specific high school graduation requirements but also both of their responsibilities toward meeting those requirements.

ADDRESSING STUDENT NEEDS

Jean Mizer tells of a haunting experience with Cliff Evans, a student who depicted her as his favorite teacher. While describing Cliff as a lonely, forgotten child, Ms. Mizer struggled. She couldn't remember much about him. She shares the consequences:

The boy lurched out of the bus, reeled, stumbled, and collapsed on the snowbank at the curb. The bus driver and I reached him at the same moment. His thin, hollow face was white even against the snow.

"He's dead," the driver whispered.

It didn't register for a minute; I glanced quickly at the scared young faces staring down at us from the school bus. "A doctor! Quick! I'll phone from the hotel . . ."

"No use; I tell you, he's dead." The driver looked down at the boy's still form.

"He never even said he felt bad," he muttered. "Just tapped me on the shoulder and said, real quiet, 'I'm sorry. I have to get off at the hotel.' That's all. Polite and apologizing like."

Cliff Evans had silently come through the school door in the mornings and gone out the school door in the evenings, and that was all. He had never been anybody at all. How do you go about making a boy a zero? I couldn't shake it. In my mind, he kept walking after me, a little boy with a peaked, pale face; a skinny body in faded jeans; and big eyes that had looked and searched for a long time and then became veiled. *You're nothing, Cliff Evans.* "A child is a believing creature." (in Dallmann-Jones, 2006, pp. 25–26)

***

Student needs are overwhelming. Continuation schools serve students and families living in adverse conditions throughout all adolescent populations, and program design would do well to include relevant, effective interventions to meet the many overwhelming demands:

- Over 1,000,000 of the 3,092,000 children reported for child abuse and neglect to the CPS agencies are verified in the United States each year, and one can only guess how many go unreported or are true but lack verification. Without a doubt, the actual numbers of abused and neglected children are much higher.
- 13,500,000 children live in poverty—about one in five (18.9 percent).
- 512,000 babies are born to teen mothers each year.
- 2,100,000 children are arrested each year.
- An estimated 1,600,000 children in the United States have an imprisoned father, and 200,000 have an imprisoned mother. Most children with incarcerated parents live in poverty before, during, and after their parents' incarceration.
- In 1999, 26 percent of twelfth-graders, 22 percent of tenth-graders, and 12 percent of eighth-graders had used illicit drugs in the previous thirty days.

- In 1999, 31 percent of twelfth-graders, 26 percent of tenth-graders, and 15 percent of eighth-graders reported having five or more alcoholic beverages in a row in the previous two-week period.
- Every five hours in the United States, another youth commits suicide. Besides the tragic loss of another young individual, the act of suicide itself devastatingly impacts dozens of friends and relatives left behind. (Dallmann-Jones, 2006, pp. 45–46)

Continuation school program design must understand the many adaptive personality traits students from adverse backgrounds use as protective factors against abusive and/or life-threatening environments. Often, continuation students are infected with what Dallmann-Jones refers to as a *Shadow Child Syndrome*: "a condition that occurs as a direct result of being raised by anyone other than nurturing caregivers."

Adolescents struggling against inimical conditions often develop:

- senses of control over their emotions, thoughts, and behaviors (through suppression and denial) as they attempt to control their worlds
- emotional avoidances as they've learned emotions are untrustworthy
- behavioral developments that block their abilities to grieve
- guilty feelings that often require them to take care of others, stir things up because calm and stable environments feel deadened or filled with boredom
- feelings of inadequacy and confusion as they search out normalcy
- attitudes that say, "The truth is, no matter what I do, I am not good enough"
- damaging patterns of behavior as they "suffer psychological pains of being alienated from their true selves which is one of the most intense, confusing, and enduring pains possible"
- distorted senses of external and internal boundaries. (pp. 81–84)

Dallmann-Jones tells us that students living with and among unfavorable conditions need to first acknowledge their personal struggles, then realize they can heal them. They need to learn how to express their pain. They need to learn from a healthy model about how to go about setting limits and boundaries for themselves in society. Schools need to reflect this model.

According to conclusions reached by the U.S. Department of Education (2010), meeting student needs includes:

- rethinking the length and structure of the school day and year
- supporting innovative models that provide the services kids need
- teacher collaboration regularly occurring to meet current and future academic challenges

- helping students to be safe, healthy, and supported in their classrooms
- offering greater opportunities to engage families in their kids' educations
- providing full-service community schools, and/or services before and after school as well as during the summer. (p. 32)

Bridgeland, DiIulio, and Burke-Morison (2006) describe an interaction between a teacher and student as the primary determinant necessary for meeting student needs:

> A great teacher can make the difference between a student who achieves at high levels and a student who slips through the cracks; and a great principal can help teachers succeed as part of a strong, well-supported instructional team. Research shows that top-performing teachers can make a dramatic difference in the achievement of their students, and suggests that the impact of being assigned to top-performing teachers year after year is enough to significantly narrow achievement gaps. (p. 13)

STRENGTHENING TEACHING

Wolk (2011) tells us that high-quality teachers show themselves by defying the odds and breaking through the barriers of distrust and disinterest—challenging and inspiring students, nourishing their curiosities, and demonstrating over and over that teaching is an act of love.

When strengthening teacher quality, therefore, it seems befitting to strengthen an array of qualities to invigorate an array of teachers. As such, personalizing teacher attributes may well be a beginning step in personalizing their teaching qualities:

> To help motivate [teachers] and maximize their abilities, we must educate them one at a time and tailor their education to their interests and needs. The engine of a new-schools strategy is personalized education. It shapes virtually every aspect of schooling. [Teachers] might play a significant role in designing their own curriculum which usually emphasizes real-world learning. They could become advisors, guiding students in educating themselves, tutoring them, and helping them manage their time and energy. [Teachers] could be assessed on the basis of actual student work as demonstrated in portfolios, exhibitions, special projects, and experiments, recitals, and performances—real accomplishments rather than abstract test scores. That's it in a nutshell. (p. 101)

Why then do we not follow similar pedagogy to strengthen teacher quality? Changes that produced significant improvements in teacher attitudes toward school and in their abilities to institute radical changes in the service of students were reported in 1996 by Wang, Haertel, and Walberg when discussing Oxley's (1994) work with small unit schools:

In an inner-city comprehensive high school and a middle school that examined the feasibility and effects of implementing small unit organization to improve student engagement, curriculum articulation across disciplines, and cross-disciplinary collaboration and collegiality among school staff was studied. Findings suggested that the following interventions meet the small unit organizational feasibility and effectiveness requirements:

- bringing about a consistent pattern of changes that modify the school culture
- implementing coordinated approaches to organizing school resources
- establishing a staff development that focuses on developing strategies and expertise for meeting the diverse needs of students. (in Almeida, Le, Steinberg, & Cervantes, 2010, p. 9)

The development of high-quality teachers is now a central focus of both federal and philanthropic efforts to improve schools nationwide. This attention should be extended to the realm of alternative education in which teachers need to be exceptionally skilled in multiple areas because of the unique demands of their field.

Alternative education teachers must possess strong knowledge of all the core academic subjects, as well as be adept at differentiating instruction and designing interdisciplinary curricula. They also must know how to combine academic challenge with supports for struggling learners—all the while engaging students who, by definition, have been the most difficult to engage.

Continuation schools serve students and their families who often dream of graduating with their classes, yet anticipate dropping out. As evidence presents a disproportionate percentage of impoverished and racially diverse adolescents making up continuation school populations, program design would do well to incorporate strength-based asset-focused factors that take this evidence into account.

***

Boykin and Noguera (2011) introduce an interpersonal relationship, asset-focused factor effective at overcoming adversities referred to as Teacher-Student Relationship Quality (TSRQ). Asset focus factors involve learning exchanges that build on the assets students bring into the classroom that provide conditions allowing these assets to flourish.

Influences of Teacher-Student Relationship Quality (TSRQ) on K–3 educational qualities that *bounce back* to classroom instructional traits established in those early years are presented here in a [bracketed] format, replacing K–3 subjects and criteria with those of secondary alternative schools to ignite reader thought, study, and evaluation:

> The level of TSRQ directly affects the level of student classroom engagement. Teacher-Student Relationship Quality—indicated by factors such as the presence of close, warm, and nurturing interactions with positive verbal exchanges and the absence of oppositional interactions that are marked by argumentation and negative exchanges and gestures—directly affects [alternative students'] levels of classroom participation, which is measured by student abilities to cooperate, follow classroom directives, and display independent, self-directed behaviors. Perceived quality of teacher-student relationships positively relates to student engagement, which in turn predicts [academic achievement assessments] in the first year [of alternative school enrollment]. Moreover, student engagement levels from the first year predicted [rigorous achievement gains] in the second year. (Boykin & Noguera, 2011, pp. 73–74)

Evidence demonstrating intrinsic limitations found among practitioners' uses of TSRQ, however, demands caution. Cultural diversity among white and black student populations produces varying responses to adult stakeholder interactions:

> More than 1,600 black and white middle school respondents from diverse socio-economical backgrounds were asked, "Whom do you most want to please with your class work?" Seventy-two percent of black students answered that they want to please their teacher. This was only the case for 30 percent of white respondents. Among these students, the most common response was "their parents." This pattern suggests that many black students don't just learn from their teachers, they also learn *for* their teachers. (Casteel, 1997, in Boykin & Noguera, 2011, p. 76)

Boykin and Noguera further Casteel's findings by discussing those of a multivariate path analytic study conducted by Tucker, Zayco, Herman, Reinke, Trujillo, Carraway, Wallack, and Ivery (2002), who looked at black students from low-income backgrounds in first through twelfth grades.

Tucker's team found a direct relationship between classroom engagement and student recognition that their teachers care about them and their academic performances, more so than with their white classmates. Strategies, however commonly differ. Irvine (1990) and Ware (2006), for example, found that a teaching approach known as *warm-demander pedagogy* is often effective primarily with black students. This method involves reprimanding students who don't live up to expectations. It shows compassion, unyielding support, and nurturance.

Studies suggest, however, that concerns acknowledge a significant limitation tied to this asset, not the least of which was discovered by Ladd, Birch, and Buhs (1999), who concluded that TSRQ is problematic for many black and Latino children.

They found that TSRQ among primary-level, K–3 students varies as a function of racial background. Evidence disclosed that white and affluent children formed closer, more positive emotional relationships and fewer conflict-ridden relationships with their teachers. Those same white and affluent youngsters were also more accepted by their classroom peers (as rated by teachers) than were their poor, black, and Latino peers.

The quality of teacher-student relationships is measurably lower for black students than it is for their white and Latino classmates. Lacking evidence as to the effects of TSRQ upon fourth-through-twelfth-grade-level black and Latino students supports further discussion in Chapter 7 of this work, "Classroom Engagement."

Asset-focused factors found in classroom dynamics encompassed in TSRQ include:

- the degree to which teachers display empathy, support, encouragement, and optimism
- the degree to which they are perceived to be fair, genuine, and nonpatronizing in their praise and feedback. (Boykin & Noguera, 2011, p. 70)

Simply put, strengthening teaching is strengthening teacher-student relationship quality so long as all children enjoy equitable degrees of the asset.

SUMMARY

Strengthening curriculum and instruction is rooted in a cultural attitude of "We as a school, can," a schoolwide sense of stakeholder efficacy built upon academic optimism and a shared belief that academic achievement is important and believed to be at the root of all schoolwide success.

A student's belief in his or her ability to succeed in school produces a learning effect influenced by individual and collective mind-sets on a school's culture demonstrated by positive outcomes for learning. While teachers are the most celebrated student supports, site-level administrators maintain the strongest influence over their school's mind-set, through supportive collegial leadership rather than directive and restrictive policies and interactions.

Effective and meaningful school reframing requires educational decision makers to think more about what should be taught and why. Researchers have learned that program design should be built upon an ethnographic platform that strengthens and defines a school's purpose to determine, examine, convey, question, and modify knowledge. Schools should improve instruction in the knowledge and attitudes that contribute to society and to provide education that reflects such. To meet this challenge, schools should give importance to basic skills and workplace values.

School design most often competes with social forces, with social forces prevailing. Effective school program design, therefore, invokes a questioning of student choice, a factor existing in spite of existing design. Student *choice* exposes student *wants*, which measure academic motivators, thereby generate empirical findings that benefit student growth.

Continuation student wants are often born from protective factors created to defend against abusive and/or life-threatening environments. A school design effective for educating students living with and among unfavorable conditions needs to first acknowledge their students' personal struggles, then realize they can heal them by recognizing their pains and providing students with a healthy model about how to go about setting limits and boundaries for themselves in which to be successful in their environments.

High-quality teachers show themselves by breaking through barriers of distrust and interest—challenging and inspiring students, nourishing their curiosities, and demonstrating over and over that teaching is an act of love. Strengthening teaching is strengthening teacher-student relationship qualities so long as all children enjoy equitable degrees of the asset.

Restructuring curriculum when supported by an inclusive, stable, and supportive learning environment can promote healthy learning for all students, comprehensive and alternative alike. Simply put, rigorous learning is built upon a high percentage of time devoted to academically focused tasks. Rigor stretches students' minds, engages their bodies and souls, and makes them want to get up in the morning and learn something new. It creates challenge. And it's most effective when centered upon students' actual experiences.

Effective school design creates a school connectedness, a belief held by students that adults and peers in their school care about their learning as well as their persons.

Chapter Six

Interventions and Methodologies

Struggling student performances often accompany struggling parent concerns. No one knows that better than Merari's parents, who see no reason for her to be in school. Merari was contemplating their concerns while helping her mom pull her screaming, three-year old brother out of the bathtub. A glance at her living room window noticed someone approaching her front door. She felt a rush of panic. She couldn't believe her teacher was at her house, unannounced.

"What is he doing here?" Merari's mind exploded. "Am I in trouble? What have I done?"

The broken doorbell forced Mr. Ramos to knock. Merari froze. Her baby brother, unaware of Mr. Ramos's intrusion, continued his screaming as Mom told Merari to throw her a towel, then answer it.

The three-year-old momentarily reduced his screaming. Merari heard a second set of knocks as she slowly approached the door while attempting to ignore her mom's yells over the baby's screams: "Merari! Responde que maldita puerta! Tengo mass manos llenas!" Merari was praying that Mr. Ramos had not heard all the yelling and screaming as she gently opened the door. Merari kept her head down with her eyes drawn upward, appearing to ask, "Why are you here? What have I done?"

Mr. Ramos's eyes sparkled. "Hi, Merari! I'm so glad you're home. Is your mom . . . ?" Merari's little brother continued his outbursts as Mr. Ramos offered to drop by at another time.

"No . . . no, really," Merari replied. "My mom'll be done putting my little brother down in a moment. Can I help you with anything?"

"You can," said Mr. Ramos. "I'd like to talk to your folks about you and school and I'd like you to be involved."

"Uh, yea. But is there anything I've done? Am I in trouble? My parents don't know . . . "

"Merari . . . que está aquí?" her mom interrupted as she walked quickly toward the conversation while wiping her hands on her apron.

"Es mi maestro, mamá. Ella quiere hablar contigo," Merari explained.

"¡Oh, tu maestro! ¿Por qué no dices algo, Merari? Mi casa es un desastre. Oh, por favor, por favor, venga y tome asiento. Merari, nos introducen. Preséntanos!"

"Mr. Ramos, this is my mom, Mrs. Sanchez. Mamá, este es mi maestra, la señor Ramos."

"Hi, Mrs. Sanchez. I'm so excited to finally get to meet you! Merari is a fantastic student and I came by to ask for your help in learning what you and your family have done to create such a wonderful young lady," Mr. Ramos said in an exuberant manner.

Merari translated, then beamed almost as much as her mom did.

***

Effective intervention and methodology applications require an awareness of student cultural values especially in a continuation school setting. Home visits can generate not only schoolwide and classroom effectiveness but the development of a full-service school as well. Home visits assist schools and their support organizations in helping students' families meet personal, basic needs, which often include livable housing, food, medical attention, and in some cases, safety.

Home visits should and can be part of a teacher's and/or administrator's job description. They go far beyond classroom effectiveness. Home visits strengthen families by, first, bringing them together to support one another and, second, connecting them with community resources.

Home visits that deliver strength-based positive supports between students and parents build a powerful trust between school and home:

> Trust is the essential building block in positive relationships that foster authentic school improvement. "Trust is what makes it happen for us," stated one parent. Trust between the school and the families it serves develops a learning environment improvement as parents, families, and community members begin to *feel listened to*. Effective schools operate full-service schools, hire school/family/community liaisons, offer adult mentoring, connect the school and community through service learning, conduct home visits, ensure effective two way communication between the school and the family, and use the school as a community center. (Parrett & Budge, 2012, pp. 126–27)

Parrett and Budge discuss Kentucky's Mason County School District, which reported a 50 percent drop in discipline referral rates along with significant increases in student attendance by simply putting into place an annual, per-pupil home visitation program. It completes what the district describes as a "whatever-it-takes" attitude.

Effective links between students' homes and schools include:

- dual-language classes for students and parents along with English as a second language classes for students
- home-school liaisons with fluency in the home language
- preschool and early literacy programs
- early assessments
- community and school activities and events. (Sadowski, 2004, in Parrett & Budge, 2012, p. 127)

Full-service schools can serve as safety nets for students struggling with adverse living conditions. They provide studentwide services such as on-site social workers, physicians, dentists, vision and hearing specialists, and mental health and family counselors. Some schools provide a childcare center and a family resource center to help families meet basic needs. Studies are looking at full-service schools that produce student attendance and achievement increases while decreasing suspension and special education placements (Dryfoos, 1994; Dryfoos & Maguire, 2002).

***

Boykin and Noguera (2011) teach that understanding student culture matters. The researchers discuss the works of Ladson-Billings (1995, 2002), who provides evidence of the effectiveness of infusing culturally relevant pedagogy into classroom practices. She teaches that once faculty members develop an understanding of the effects of home visits on their culturally diverse students and families, understandings become a part of their classroom instruction. Teachers raise *community-based* issues that exemplify challenges that students and their families face in their everyday lives.

Teachers amplify the rigor of their lessons by urging students, in age-appropriate ways, to "confront the realities of power and privilege in the larger society or link events that happen in their lives to the school's official curriculum" (Parrett & Budge, 2012, p. 127).

Gonzalez, Moll, and Amanti (2005) offer another culturally relevant intervention:

> [Faculty and staff] draw upon the funds of knowledge to be found in students' family and community experiences. The ultimate goal of this approach is to create greater experiential familiarity among teachers, students, and their families. Teachers in effect, engage in ethnographic research in their students'

communities to learn about the knowledge, skills and assets that can be discovered. (p. 103)

Peer mentoring is yet another effective intervention. Jackson (2002) mentions four positive outcomes of mentoring programs:

- personalizing attention and care
- accessing resources
- offering positive/high expectations for staff and students
- building reciprocity, active youth participation, and commitment. (in Parrett & Budge, 2012, p. 127)

Among the most widely researched and empirically successful collaborative learning methods is classwide peer tutoring (CWPT), which operates by randomly assigning students to two teams within the classroom and then randomly assigning students to pairs (within the teams).

Students in each pair alternate playing the roles of tutor and tutored. Typically, the learning activities are scripted and structured by the teacher so that instructions can be easily followed, regardless of a student's skill level. Students accrue points for their team by answering questions correctly. CWPT is especially useful for reinforcing and practicing basic academic skills.

***

Numbered Heads Together is yet another successful peer-assisted learning activity. Students participate in mixed-skill groups of four with each member randomly assigned a number. First, the teacher poses a question. She then provides enough time for students in their groups to pose an agreed-upon response. The teacher randomly calls upon group members by number to provide their response to the class.

Group members ensure that every member understands the material as each group member's response reflects upon the group's capability as a whole (Maheady, Mallette, Harper, & Sacca, 1991; Kagan, 1992).

Student engagement drives academic growth. Adaptive asset-focused factors gathered from student engagement observation data direct the required levels of engagement that leads to desired outcomes. Assets address any personal, social, cultural, experiential, and intellectual capital that students from diverse backgrounds bring to the table. Prominent among the guiding functions of such assets are self-efficacy, self-regulated learning, and incremental beliefs about intelligence or ability. Student achievement is directly related to these functions.

METHODOLOGIES

Continuation faculty room discussions frequently argue classroom methodologies, interactions, and interventions. Research findings rarely, if ever, enter into their arguments. During one such discussion, a question arose as to why faculty members defend their methodologies so vehemently. One contributor's response: "Because we teach the way we were taught. We always have . . . what's wrong with that?" The response exposes a keystone barrier to methodological change.

***

Nelson, Palonsky, and McCarthy (2007) offer a look at challenging this roadblock through a dialectic reasoning intervention designed to unite varying classroom methodologies for the purpose of forming a united, school-wide academic program.

Dialectic reasoning examines opposing ideas for the purpose of developing one creative and superior idea, a level beyond simple dialogue (Sim, 1999; Farrar, 2000; Sciabarra, 1999).

It promotes critical thinking.

Dialectic reasoning avoids defeating opposing or divergent ideas in favor of searching for an improved idea. "It is a search for a higher level of idea that accommodates or incorporates the most important points in the thesis and antithesis" (Nelson, Palonsky, & McCarthy, 2007, p. 8).

It's an existing intervention, somewhat common among safety-net continuation schools with far-reaching academic possibilities. Mr. Ramos and Jonathan's discussion exemplifies the point.

***

It began when Jonathan felt unsure. He had somehow, somewhere, lost control over his relationship with everyone at the school. He didn't know where he stood. He started jogging to and from school to calm himself down. It's not like he hated people here; it's like he didn't or couldn't understand them and that can't happen for Jonathan.

He noticed some students just sitting around campus, talking with their advisors, so he asked Mr. Ramos, his advisor, if he would give him a moment just before lunch. During their conversation, something happened that reminded Jonathan of talks he used to have with Dr. Williams at his old school.

"See," Jonathan began. "I used to know this kid that lived two doors down. Everyone said he was ganging, you know, a gang-banger. Me and him used to smoke down by the railroad tracks that were close to the projects, you know, where we lived. Anyways, this kid talked a lot about gangin'. Said they were all close, real close, you know, like family. They'd do anything for each other, know what I mean? Even kill, you know, if they had to. Yea. And nobody, I mean nobody could break any of 'em apart."

"That's just the way it is," he continued. "When you got somebody's back, it's called *committed*, you know, for both of you. You know, havin' somebody's back, that's all there is. There ain't nothin' else, know what I mean? It's like family, that's what family is. No matter what ... yea."

When Mr. Ramos asked Jonathan what it would be like if his school had his back, you know, sort of like his friend's gang, he slowly looked away. Mr. Ramos overheard him mumble to himself, "Yea, right. Whoever heard of a school that gots your back? Still ... What if ... Yea?"

***

Dialectic reasoning *anchors* idea variations to both dualistic and monistic thoughts. "The dialectic thinker refuses to recognize these camps as mutually exclusive or apparent opposites. He or she strives to uncover the common roots of apparent opposites and presents an integrated alternative" (Sciabarra, 1999, in Nelson, Palonsky, & McCarthy, 2007, p. 9).

School is important enough to examine argument, according to Nelson's study team, and as such, dialogue and dialectic, used in an anchoring way, are intended to be dynamic, interactive, and optimistic. Dialogue and dialectic are optimistic since they take the stance that things can and should be improved. Supportive, longitudinal evidence substantiates Nelson, Palonsky, and McCarthy's arguments:

> While dialogue merely calls for two persons or two ideas, reasoned dialogue involves active consideration of different views and interests in confabulatory interactions. Dialogue does not expect much beyond civil discussion used to gain understanding. Dialectic reasoning uses disputes and divergent opinions to arrive at a better idea. The dialectic occurs when you pit one argument (thesis) against another (antithesis) in an effort to develop a synthesis superior to either. It is an inquiry into important issues that identifies the main points, important evidence, and logical arguments used by each of at least two divergent views on an issue. This requires critical examination of the evidence and arguments on each side of a dispute, granting each side some credibility to understand and criticize. A dialectic approach is dynamic. A synthesis from one level of dialectic reasoning can become a new thesis at a more sophisticated level and the process of inquiry continues to spiral. (Adler, 1927; Cooper, 1967; Rychlak, 1976; Noddings, 1995; Blumenfeld-Jones, 2004, in Nelson, Palonsky, & McCarthy, 2007, p. 8)

Wang, Haertel, and Walberg (1994) teach that schoolwide foundational building blocks necessary to create effective classroom methodologies include:

- faculties and staffs believing that all students can succeed
- schools having stable, intimate, and collegial contexts for teaching and learning
- decentralizing systems of school management with a staff having greater authority and flexibility
- parents having access to school staff more readily
- coherent academic programs
- all teachers sharing a sense of responsibility for student success
- a school staff having access to the knowledge base on effective classroom and schoolwide practices and systemic reform strategies
- schools employing systematic, site-based professional development. (p. 10)

Examples of effective intervention and methodology program design are found in the following programs reported by Dianda (2008) for the National Education Association:

- *Achievement for Latinos through Academic Success (ALAS)* is a middle school intervention designed to affect dropping out. In the ALAS program, each student is assigned a counselor who monitors attendance, behavior, and academic achievement. The counselor provides feedback and coordinates communication among students, families, and teachers. Counselors also serve as advocates for students and intervene when problems are identified. Students are trained in problem-solving skills, and parents are trained in parent-child problem solving, how to participate in school activities, and how to contact teachers and school administrators when issues arise. http://www.promisingpractices.net/program.asp
- *Accelerated Middle Schools* are self-contained academic programs designed to help middle school students who are behind grade level catch up with their age peers. These programs serve students who are one to two years behind grade level. Current evidence is not provided as to their effectiveness at increasing attendance and high school graduation. http://ies.ed.gov/ncee/wwc/reports/dropout/ams/index.asp
- *Career Academies* consist of small learning communities (150 to 200 students), often located within large high schools in low-income, urban areas. The academies combine a college preparatory curriculum with technical and occupational courses and team with local businesses to provide students with after-school, career-related learning opportunities. The goal is to keep students interested in school by demonstrating how their coursework will help them with employment. Approved applicants enter an academy in their first year of high school and are taught by a single team of teachers through grade twelve. http://www.ncacinc.org

- *Middle College High Schools* are alternative high schools located on college campuses that focus on helping at-risk students complete high school and encouraging them to attend college. The schools offer a project-centered, interdisciplinary curriculum, with an emphasis on team teaching, individualized attention, and the development of critical thinking skills. http://www.mcnc.us
- *New Chance* is a program for young mothers who have dropped out of school. It is designed to improve both their employment potential and their parenting skills. Participants take GED preparation classes and complete a parenting and life skills curriculum. http://www.newchance.org/
- *Quantum Opportunity Program* is an extensive, comprehensive program that offers case management, mentoring, tutoring, and other education and support services. It also offers financial incentives for participation in program activities. Participants enter the program in the ninth grade and can receive services for four to five years, even if they drop out. http://www.promisingpractices.net/
- *Talent Development High Schools* is a reform model for restructuring struggling large high schools into small *learning communities*—including ninth-grade academies and career academies—to reduce student isolation and anonymity. They report incorporating high academic standards in all coursework while providing all students with a college preparatory academic curriculum. http://www.csos.jhu/tdhs
- *Jobs for America's Graduates (JAG)* uses a trained career specialist, who is often a teacher, who works with thirty-five to forty-five students who have been identified by a school-based committee as being at high risk of dropping out of school. JAG offers students a curriculum that focuses on employability competencies, adult mentoring and advice, and student-led leadership development, all with a twelve-month follow-up once students graduate or complete their GED (pp. 79–82). http://www.jag.org

INSTRUCTIONAL DESIGN CRITERIA

Observations and faculty room discussions show that many teachers use instructional designs they recall as being their favorites during their student experiences. As a result, significant numbers of struggling students are denied opportunities to discover their own personal strategies, resulting, so often, tragically.

To offset this risk, alternative teachers need to become aware of instructional designs successful at meeting the needs of all their students, without the benefits of research. Ruiz de Velasco and McLaughlin (2012) tell us why:

> Our study of alternative schools in California has focused on learning about policy variables at the state, district, and community levels that mediate stu-

dent outcomes in individual schools. We have not spent sufficient time in schools and classrooms to make informed recommendations about the detailed *instructional* aspects of [continuation] school level change. (p. 20)

Lacking evidence suggests that no one else has either. As such, the following researchers and authors offer educational constructs that may well provide foundations for effective continuation school instruction that allows for and supports individual student-centered instructional design.

***

Effective instructional frameworks are built upon foundations of academic optimism and student achievement, say the authors, despite student SES. Schools must drive toward rigorous classroom achievement in an atmosphere of support, built upon academic optimism. To accomplish this task, instructional design would do well to inject community features into their classroom instructional strategies.

Data analyzed by Kirby and DiPaola in their study, *Academic Optimism and Achievement: A Path Model* (2009), concluded that "there is a significant relationship between the community engagement dimension of school climate and academic optimism, and between academic optimism and student achievement" (p. 80). The researchers found that student gains are a function of academic optimism, which is also a function of an open, healthy school. Simply put, parents and teachers working together produce a higher student achievement level, resulting in a "We can" school atmosphere.

"Mobilizing the community at large and forming partnerships with schools can have a positive impact on student achievement," say Henderson and Mapp (2002). An example includes leadership going as far as employing parents to build a bridge between family and home.

An effective instructional framework built upon a foundation of academic optimism, student achievement, and community engagement addresses another condition that creates a challenging and rigorous instructional framework: an efficacious academic environment. "Collective teacher efficacy represents the judgment of the teachers regarding the extent to which they as a whole can cause a particular outcome" (Kirby & DiPaola, 2009, p. 84).

Self-efficacy can be advanced through mastery and vicarious experiences, social persuasion, and modeling, all of which establish an instructional core affecting the way a teacher perceives a school (Bandura, 1997; Goddard, Hoy, & Woolfolk-Hoy, 2004).

> In the broadest sense, an instructional framework consists of the theories, policies, structures, processes, and practices used in a school to guide what happens in the classroom—the dynamic interaction between content, student, and teacher contributing to an *instructional core*. Constructs that influence an

instructional core include a common vision of what teaching excellence looks like . . . aligning curriculum with state and district standards . . . selecting and using research-based instructional practices and . . . developing and using common assessments. (Parrett & Budge, 2012, p. 151)

Several schools studied by the authors adopted a Comprehensive School Reform model customized to address their identified student needs. Using a research-based defense for the suggested instructional practices, participating schools implemented curricular materials derived from formative and summative assessments. Evidence provided by the researchers suggest a list of schoolwide practices that fit well with a continuation school instructional framework:

- bonding students with their school through class meetings, homeroom advisories, placements in higher-level courses, and offering athletics and clubs all foster a sense of belonging
- developing critical-thinking skills that include higher-order questioning, problem-based learning, Socratic seminars, and multidisciplinary units
- providing opportunities to build short-term working memory through multisensory instruction and memory aids (mnemonic devices)
- providing specific opportunities for the development of social skills through cooperative learning, peer tutoring, and mentoring
- accessing and building upon prior knowledge to further knowledge through brainstorming, semantic mapping, advance organizers, tuning and reconstruction. and autobiographical activities
- mediating and scaffolding learning experiences through reciprocal teaching, "think-alouds," visual organizers/models, guided practice, and shelter instruction
- meeting diverse learning needs through personalizing instruction based upon student learning styles, multiple intelligences, differentiated instruction, and tiered structures for learning
- accelerating and enriching rather than remediating learning through developing student talent, college-prep course offerings, advanced placement/honors, and arts education for all
- engaging students in learning experiences for authentic, meaningful purposes by offering project-based learning activities, place-based learning assignments, and authentic assessments
- connecting physical activity, exercise, and motor development to learning by offering PE-focused lifelong sports and fitness learnings, schoolwide fitness goals, and progress monitoring and sensory motor labs
- providing learning experiences that help students envision their futures and foster hope through service learning, community-based internships, and mentoring. (pp. 160–61)

STUDENT MISBEHAVIOR STRATEGIES

Instructional framework design would do well to include student misbehavior into its schoolwide learning criteria, associating it with the curriculum. As relevancy takes hold of learning, perceived benefits from the misbehavior are replaced with actual classroom achievement and success, often resulting in respect and recognition. To avoid misbehavior altogether, however, Henderson and Milstein (2003) purport building an atmosphere of consistent student recognition throughout all instructional activities.

The authors discuss an "On a Roll" program, whereby school staff recognizes students who improve over the term in academic work, behavior, and/or attendance. During a school assembly, these students and their parents are honored as being *on a roll* to success. Some schools have extended the "On a Roll" concept to businesses and organizations as they recognize student contributions to their communities as well:

> Students generate a list of attractive awards like free movie tickets, free meals in fancy restaurants, a limousine ride, and discounts at local businesses. All students who bring their grades up one grade point or improve attendance in a semester are publicly recognized for their work and their names are placed in a drawing for the coveted prizes. Limousines pulling up to the school to take students to local restaurants for lunchtime meals, as the student body looks on, demonstrate the creativity of a staff. (pp. 97–98)

Student misbehavior can be reddressed as a positive learning experience when studying instructional framework constructs. Henderson and Milstein further their thoughts by offering a framework for strengthening a student's self-esteem when confronting his or her inappropriate behavior through the use of "referral forms that include equal space for identifying problems and strengths to help ensure that a student's strengths are looked at in equal proportion to the risks or problems" (p. 98).

Conflict-resolution programs can also strengthen appropriate student behavior. As students and staff are trained in a conflict-resolution curriculum, certain students can act as conflict mediators:

> Students in mediation classes are available every period of a school day to mediate conflicts between their peers at school. Conflict resolution programs produce a 95% rate of students keeping the agreements they reached. Because a mediation process involves the disputants listening to one another, hearing one another's points of view, and coming up with a mutually agreed-upon solution in a five-step process facilitated by mediators, it builds resiliency for all involved. Students began mediating neighborhood and family conflicts, based on their experiences at school, causing numerous parents to contact the schools requesting mediation training for themselves. (p. 100)

Henderson and Milstein discuss a Process of Conflict Mediation requiring mediators to first explain the roles and rules of meditation, followed by:

- defining the problem—parties describe their view of the situation and express their feelings
- mediators helping parties to understand one another's points of view
- parties finding a solution through mediators helping parties brainstorm and deciding on a solution agreeable to both
- mediators writing down the points agreed-upon, including all participant signatures. (New Mexico Center for Dispute Resolution)

Students are resources, rather than users of resources. As resources, students are "actively engaged in learning rather than passively receiving someone else's knowledge; producing rather than consuming; offering help rather than always receiving help; and serving as leaders rather than followers or victims" (Henderson & Milstein, 2003, p. 102).

***

"I need your help, Merari," Mr. Ramos said. "See that new kid, Jose, over there, sitting at that back table? Do you know him?"

"Uh, no . . . don't think so, Mr. Ramos," she replied.

"He struggles with English. So did I when I was his age. I think I know how he feels. He told me about an essay he wants to write, one that's important to him, but he doesn't know enough English. As he told me about it, I inserted some words I thought would be helpful, but he looked away. I think he's intimidated because I'm his teacher. That happens with some kids. You think you might try?"

"Sure. I'll sit next to him and do my work. Maybe we can strike up a conversation." Merari picked up her books and slowly wandered over to a seat across from Jose. Mr. Ramos noticed the beginning of a cautious discussion.

Toward the end of class, Jose had a stack of pages in front of him while still working on another. Merari was sitting across from him, quietly working on her future presentation. Mr. Ramos was mystified. How'd she do that?

"Merari, can I see you for a moment?"

"Sure, Mr. Ramos," she answered.

"It was simple, Mr. Ramos," she began. "Jose knew what he wanted to say, just not in English. So I told him to write his essay in Spanish. When he got through, I promised to carefully go through it with him, helping him to translate his paper into English. He really got excited. He said he could learn a lot more English that way. So tomorrow, after he finishes his paper tonight for homework, we'll work together to translate it. Yea?"

A MULTIPLE PATHWAYS APPROACH TO CURRICULUM DESIGN

A Multiple Pathways approach to learning is seen as "a multiyear, comprehensive high school program of integrated academic and technical study that is organized around a broad theme, interest area, or industry sector" (CDE, 2010, p. 13). As *choice* provides evidence of student trust resulting in degrees of respect shown among continuation school stakeholders, a Multiple Pathways strategy strengthens rigorous learning via student choice opportunities. It can be argued, therefore, that *choice*, as an inclusive construct, strengthens program development.

As with comprehensive high schools, a continuation school pathway design can provide a selection of curricular pathways, tied to professions and careers that are available throughout professional jurisdictions, with each pathway aligned to one or more industry sectors. The purpose offers students access to at least one career-level pathway that promotes their interests by supporting them in selecting their high school or course of study.

Regardless of any chosen pathway, rigor embodies all academic studies and career technical courses, work-based learning, and support services so as to maximize high school learning supported by postgraduate career choices (CDE, 2010).

A multipathways design is strengthened when each pathway embodies the following four components:

- an integrated core curriculum that provides access to a challenging academic component that prepares students for success in colleges and universities, including apprenticeships and other postsecondary programs
- an integrated career technical core curriculum, including a sequence of at least four yearlong related courses that contain Career Technical Education (CTE) standards-based courses providing students with career management skills and are aligned with and underscore core academic principles and standards
- a series of work-based learning opportunities that begin with mentoring, job shadowing, and evolve into intensive internships, school-based enterprises, or electronically assisted mentorships
- student support services to help students master the advanced academic and career technical content. (CDE, 2010, p. 14)

Student interest and desire to learn are both key components in initiating learning through active participation. Because pathways learning is designed to help students understand the relevance of their learning experiences beyond school, it offers a schoolwide curriculum shift benefiting students through the following components:

- smaller school environments allowing students to be known by their teachers, peers, and other school staff, all of which develop a sense of belonging through community
- deepening student learning through both academic and career technical skill areas, as reflected through performance-based assessments and other demonstrations of acquired knowledge and skill
- developmental appropriateness achievement through increasing levels of responsibility and autonomy as students mature
- high-quality curriculum development by teachers with expertise in their respective fields and taught through a variety of strategies, including coaching and facilitating project-based and work-based learning, in addition to instruction
- program inputs from industry and communities to inform the design and delivery of curricula and student learning experiences. (pp. 14–16)

***

For the most part, Wolk (2011) agrees with a multiple pathways approach to learning. He teaches that multiple approaches to a learning pathway should at the very least be incorporated into the high school level and coordinated with community-based education programs and children support systems.

His thoughts add that a multiple pathways school design needs to include a traditional college prep program, virtual school programs, and an effective, independent study offering. While the nature of the pathway dominates the design, Wolk argues that high academic standards must be implemented into all programs.

It is commonly accepted that skills sought by employers occur in the elementary grades—K–8, say participants of human resources discussions. Student-selected educational pathways thereafter, should be compatible with student interests, aspirations, and learning styles.

Job training is not a task of schools. "Indeed," Wolk teaches, "Employers commonly assert that if schools teach students to think and reason—to read, write, do basic math, and display good habits of conduct—[the employer] will assume the responsibility of teaching them what they need to know about a specific job" (p. 111).

SUMMARY

Home visits build awareness of family needs affecting student learning. Resulting full service schools can provide studentwide services such as on-site social workers, physicians, dentists, vision and hearing specialists, and mental health and family counselors. Some schools provide a childcare center and a family resource center to help families better meet basic needs.

While student engagement drives personal, social, and intellectual capital, *dialectic reasoning* offers an examination of opposing ideas for the purpose of creating one superior idea that goes beyond simple dialogue (Sim, 1999; Farrar, 2000; Sciabarra, 1999). It promotes critical thinking. It's an existing intervention, somewhat common among safety-net continuation schools with far-reaching academic possibilities.

Dialectic reasoning uses disputes and divergent opinions to arrive at those far-reaching possibilities. The dialectic occurs when you pit one argument against another in an effort to develop a synthesis superior to either. Greatly improved instructional frameworks can be a result.

Effective instructional frameworks are built upon foundations of academic optimism and student achievement, despite student SES. Schools must drive toward rigorous classroom achievement in an atmosphere of support, built upon academic optimism. Parents and teachers working together produce a higher student achievement level resulting in a *we can* school atmosphere.

An effective instructional framework built upon a foundation of academic optimism, student achievement, and community engagement addresses another condition necessary to create a challenging and rigorous instructional framework: an efficacious academic environment. Self-efficacy can take hold through schoolwide experiences involving social persuasion, modeling, and affective support, all of which affect the way a teacher relates to her school (Bandura, 1997; Goddard, Hoy, & Woolfolk-Hoy, 2004).

Students are resources, rather than users of resources. As resources, they are "actively engaged in learning rather than passively receiving someone else's knowledge; producing rather than consuming; offering help rather than always receiving help; and serving as leaders rather than followers or victims" (Henderson & Milstein, 2003, p. 102). A Multiple Pathways curriculum approach offers students access to at least one career-level pathway that promotes their interests by supporting them in selecting their high school or course of study.

As *choice* provides evidence of student trust resulting in degrees of respect shown among continuation school stakeholders, a Multiple Pathways strategy strengthens rigorous learning via student choice opportunities. Critical schoolwide factors encouraging student choice include caring relationships and advocacy, high expectations and support, unwavering commitments to equity, senses of professional accountability for learning, and the courage and will needed to take action.

Regardless of any chosen pathway, rigor must embody all academic studies and career technical courses, work-based learning, and support services so as to maximize high school learning supported by postgraduate career choices (CDE, 2010). A multiple pathways school design should also include a traditional college prep program, virtual school programs, and an effective independent study offering.

Chapter Seven

Classroom Engagement

Classroom engagements are studied by Fredericks, Blumenfeld, and Paris (2004) in three groups: behavioral, cognitive, and affective. Behavioral engagement deals with *on-task behaviors*—cognitive refers to *comprehending complex concepts and issues*, while affective engagement addresses *emotional reactions linked to task investment*. Simply put, the greater the interest, the greater the affective engagement.

Student engaged, on-task behavior assessments, as determiners of student achievement, are found to quell the current, age-old determiner: instructional time.

***

Bodovski and Farkas (2007) report that students with the lowest initial test scores experience the greatest amount of instructional time, yet assess at the lowest levels of achievement. Researchers further distinguish engagement from instructional time as they conclude that instructional time as a variable fails when compared to the engagement variable no matter the category of student engagement.

Research demonstrating teacher/student relationships based upon student classroom engagement levels is characterized by Greenwood (1996):

> Students who are more engaged in classroom activities receive more positive teacher attention in return; whereas unengaged students receive less positive attention and more *coercion* from teachers. Over time, the initial effect gets increasingly amplified and even ritualized or regularized. An absence of positive reinforcement and infrequent opportunities to respond, lead to lower levels of academic responding. (in Boykin & Noguera, 2011, p. 48)

Skinner and Belmont (1993) take the position that student affective engagement is found in student perceptions of teacher behaviors. Although this concern most often addresses student feelings surrounding teacher/student interaction, student observation of teacher actions takes affective engagement to higher levels.

The researchers suggest not only a student perception of teacher behavioral influence but teacher behavior being mediated by *teacher perception* of students' levels of motivation and engagement as well. A teacher might attempt to heighten a student's level of engagement, or magnify the low engagement. Simply put, the teacher may overplay the low level by exhibiting less involvement. A teacher may even unknowingly restrict any student encouragement.

***

Avoidance strategies, common among strugglers, seem to dominate factors that are the antithesis of engagement (Turner, Meyer, Anderman, Midgley, Gheen, Yongjin, & Patrick, 2002). They include self-handicapping through procrastinating, purposely not trying hard, looking for excuses not to study, avoiding help, guessing at answers rather than asking for help, not asking questions in class, and choosing to work only on familiar problems (Boykin & Noguera, 2011, p. 47).

The most critical of Skinner and Belmont's findings, however, shows that positive student engagement is built upon positive teacher behaviors. Teachers are more likely to respond to students initially demonstrating high levels of engagement. Skinner and Belmont suggest that these findings can and do permeate within a classroom while slowly building up over time.

Four pathways, according to Schunk and Zimmerman (2007), lead to self-regulatory competence, a significant classroom engagement quality: observation, emulation, self-control, and self-regulation:

> At the first level (observation), learners become acquainted with appropriate thoughts and actions by observing models that demonstrate the desired behaviors and thought processes. At the next step (emulation), learners attempt to carry out the appropriate behaviors and thought processes of the model. At the self-control level, learners have internalized the requisite thoughts and actions and in the final state (self-regulation), learners are guided by self-produced representations. (p. 57)

Classroom engagement is strongly influenced by asset-focused factors. Asset-focused factors involve learning exchanges that build on the assets students bring into the classroom. Teachers create classroom conditions that allow these assets to promote student learning. While asset features found among students appear infinite, the following are seen by the authors as commonplace:

- existing or emerging interests and preferences
- motivational inclinations
- passions and commitments
- attitudes, beliefs, opinions, self-perceptions, personal or collective identities
- prior experiences, knowledge, understanding, skills and competencies. (Boykin & Noguera, 2011, p. 197)

Teachers would do well to first identify these assets among and within their student populations through an array of activities, then incorporate them into their classroom engagement strategies.

Boykin and Noguera attempt to find out why student asset-focused features increase classroom engagement by first categorizing them into three distinct but interrelated groups, then studying the characteristics of interpersonal relationships, intersubjectivity, and information-processing quality.

Social exchanges address interpersonal relationships while intersubjectivity deals with the extent of compatibility in the interests, values, perceptions, and learning objectives of teachers and students. Information-processing quality addresses subject matter content interacting with student cognitive engagements that promote deep understanding, higher-order thinking, effective and efficient information processing, and long-term retention.

***

Emotional feedback, an effective engagement intervention, is a strong predictor of academic achievement, as well as student self-efficacy ratings (Stevens, Olivarez, & Hamming, 2006). Emotional feedback involves student praise, positive feedback, and anxiety reduction.

Present in all student responses found in the Stevens et al. study is evidence provided by Stewart (2008) suggesting that highly effective student-teacher interactions include student perceptions of getting along well with their teachers, having caring teachers, and receiving praise for good efforts. All are significant predictors of increased academic achievement.

Synthesizing the cultural conditions students bring to their classrooms with those required by academics allows practitioners to maximize the possibility that a greater number of students—from a wider range of backgrounds—will be more fully engaged and responsive to the increasingly higher-learning demands they will be expected to meet in the twenty-first century (Delpit, 1995; Hale, 2004).

Chapter 7

SELF-DETERMINATION: A SENSE OF AUTONOMY

Self-Determination Theory holds that accomplishing a challenging task and causing a desired effect motivates student engagement, which in turn builds a sense of competence leading to increased capacity (Ryan & Deci, 2000). Increased capacity generates a sense of autonomy.

"A person is autonomous when his or her behavior is experienced as willingly enacted and when he or she fully endorses the action in which he or she is engaged" (Chirkov, Ryan, Kim, & Kaplan, 2003, in Boykin & Noguera, 2011, p. 85).

Interactions that foster autonomous support include:

- empathy for the student's perspective/point of view
- a compelling rationale for involvement
- independent thinking and criticism
- choices within the limits of a given situation. (Vansteenkiste, Lens, & Deci, 2006; Vansteenkiste & Sheldon, 2006)

These behavioral traits have presented themselves among adolescent sample groups and are observed among continuation student populations.

***

Lee (2001, 2006) studied the differences between student capabilities expressed academically and under culturally familiar circumstances whereby students use reasoning, analyses, and problem-solving strategies aligned with those expected and required in academic settings, even though those same students do not typically display such skills in their classrooms with respect to academic subject matter. Vansteenkiste and Sheldon (2006) learned that while students may actually be using such strategies outside of school, they don't realize their benefits in school or classroom settings.

Academically vulnerable students using critical-thinking, problem-solving, or learning strategies to promote enhanced academic outcomes are rare. While some believe these attributes to be crucial, surely valuable classroom objectives, they are not common in continuation settings. Two examples of teaching criteria supporting them, however, are the following:

- *Adaptive learning strategies* identifies classroom activities that lead to deeper processing of subject matter by helping students recognize what they should actually do with the facts, why the right answer is correct, and what can be inferred from information on the printed page.
- *Cognitive elaboration* focuses on going beyond *yes/no* or *true/false* answers, beyond bubbling in multiple-choice responses to focusing on ena-

bling students to justify their answers, provide more thoughtful and reflective answers, and to recognize their roles as knowledge producers rather than simply knowledge consumers. (Boykin & Noguera, 2011, pp. 125–27)

Adaptive strategies include students being engaged in cooperative pairs, thereby learning more by supporting one another than by simply listening and checking for errors. "Tutors learn more than tutees," say business roundtable participants.

***

King (1992), a student of cognitive elaboration, teaches that students are more able to comprehend and recall when they are required to elaborate upon a material's content, which typically requires adding details, clarifying an idea, and/or applying an analogy.

She suggests that teachers provide students with a set of generic question stems that may be used in a variety of independent subject matter content, such as:

- What is another example of . . . ?
- What would happen if . . . ?
- What are the strengths and weaknesses of . . . ?
- What is the difference between . . . and . . . ?
- Do you agree or disagree with . . . ?
- Support your answers with evidence. (in Boykin & Noguera, 2011, p. 128)

Students offer questions independently and then pair up, asking and answering questions with a partner. This strategy leads to higher-quality representation of the relevant material and a deeper understanding of it as well. It not only allows for a greater pathway for information recall, it works well with a variety of learning formats, including lecture presentations and peer-guided, small-group discussions and independent reviews.

These learning activities lead to student ownership of questions and answers. Students own their own learning processes as well as recognize their own knowledge gaps. The teaching of generic questioning and explanation skills can direct the teaching of specific academic skills and learning strategies that are often indices of academic performance.

***

Boykin and Noguera argue as to how little or no effort is made by schools to synthesize student inferences and perceptions surrounding their everyday life experiences with what they call "explicitly induced skills in the context of formal classroom reading exercises." Hansen (1981) provided practice with two different ways of making inferences to a group of "average" students from diverse SES backgrounds while attempting to create student ownership of the engaged material.

During a five-week period, Hansen's students either practiced making inferences about assigned text passages or received a five-week prereading regimen of inferential thinking strategy training. Students:

- discussed questions that drew on their own prior experiences
- answered those questions
- discussed what story characters might do in similar settings
- offered their own hypotheses of what might happen
- repeated the first four steps
- discussed the advantage of this approach to reading. (in Boykin & Noguera, 2011, p. 133)

"If a student is deeply interested in a project created from her own chosen purpose, she will learn it because it is simply necessary to do so," Wolk (2003) tells us. In a strengths-based program, schools focus on students' strongest interests and use them as a foundation in which to build.

> At Minnesota New Country School in Henderson, Minnesota, the curriculum is built upon pursuing personal student interest. The heart of the school is project-based education. There is no curriculum, no principal; teachers run the school. Instead of traditional classrooms, each student has a workplace in an office-like setting. Every student has a computer, but books are everywhere. Students work alone or in groups, and advisors tutor individual students, often at their work stations. New Country students work with community experts and are evaluated by them on their performance. Students also evaluate themselves, using a performance rubric to rate their work in three areas: critical thinking skills, leadership and innovation, and the quality of their specific work product. (pp. 105–6)

The results are impressive. All students demonstrated equal growth of inferential as well as comprehensive reading skills. The author tells us that inference comprehension levels for poor readers at New Country increased as high as 50 percent when students received inference training.

Inferential learning, making inferences, or "reading between the lines" is benefiting educational programming at all levels.

It is often seen in related learning programs such as inquiry based, project based, hands-on, cooperative, service, career and technical, and vocational as well. Yet real-world learning is most often ignored, most surely avoided by mainstream education. The results are disturbing in light of findings by the

Horatio Alger Association of Distinguished Americans (2005) study that shows a strong majority of students believing that more real-world learning would improve their schools.

PERSONALIZING INSTRUCTION

Personalizing classroom instruction offers students opportunities at becoming a part of their own coursework. It conveys a sense of ownership, of relevance in a true sense.

While relevancy tied to liberal arts studies is seen when comparing personal experiences with those of significant historical and literary importance, the study of science or math offers a different set of ownership challenges.

In their study, "Using Computer-Assisted Instruction to Personalize Arithmetic Materials for Elementary School Children" (1987), Anand and Ross looked for reasons students see math as difficult as well as whether or not context is central to their struggles. Their concerns led to a belief that increased comprehension of a problem's demands will improve a student's ability to focus on relevant information and not only solve the problem but apply it to their own personal concerns as well.

The researchers randomly placed students into three practice/learning condition groups: (1) abstract, where problems are described in general terms; (2) concrete, where problems are presented with specific but hypothetical referents; and (3) personalized, where problem text is supported by personal information about a given student. While all conditions contained identical mathematics information and operations, the manner in which the problems were described was differed.

Two performance outcome measures were used: an immediate posttest, and a transfer measure. The researchers first offered a posttest that maintained a similar structure and challenge level as the lesson problems. They then offered a transfer measure consisting of a set of problems on the same material, but structured differently so as to create what they called "a novel format for students."

Results showed that students performed best under the personalized condition, which was stronger with the transfer outcome than the posttest outcome. Anand and Ross also showed that while students in high-level capacity groups performed similarly in the personalized and concrete conditions, those in the low-medium groups performed significantly better in the personalized condition.

"Infusing personalization into problem texts creates an increased opportunity for students to link the problem to well-known and personally interesting information, which then leads to higher performance outcomes" (Boykin & Noguera, 2011, p. 95).

***

Cordova and Lepper's (1996) work found that students who personalized information included in the problems and were encouraged to devise descriptive qualities of the actual problems retained new knowledge longer and produced more applicable results. Personalizing instruction to positively affect classroom engagement can be introduced by offering students choices of *entry points* into the subject, topic, or concept being studied. Gardner (2011) points to five:

- *Narrational* entry points are effective when a teacher uses either previous or current student essays to introduce a lesson by telling relevant, meaningful stories that fit well into an upcoming topic. Often, students are extremely effective at narrating their own stories personally to a class.
- *Logical-quantitative* entry points become apparent as students discuss controversies relevant to particular student populations. Debates, for example, arguing the merits and deficiencies of the 1973 U.S. Supreme Court decision *Roe v. Wade*, bring forth decision-making experiences familiar to pregnant teens, a student population often found in continuation schools.
- *Foundational* entry points examine philosophical and terminological facets of a concept, such as a student pondering the context of what a pastor preaches (and the language used to do so) in comparison to what his or her gang leader professes while using his chosen dialect.
- *Esthetic* approaches address sensory or surface features such as students examining the esthetic feelings they receive while sitting alone in a funeral parlor as an experience that activates an esthetic sensitivity.
- *Experiential* approaches support students' learning with a hands-on approach, working with materials that embody the subject matter.

FLOW: A MOTIVATIONAL STRATEGY

The concept of *flow* addresses a "mental state of operation in which a person performing an activity is fully immersed in a feeling of energized focus," says Csikszentmihalyi (1997). *Flow* is a feeling, an emotional testimony to the building of personal autonomy, if you will, and it can take many forms. Continuation students evidencing *flow*, however, can demonstrate results different from what a teacher may somewhat have in mind while working with a resilient student population. Kristi's essay offers such an example:

Mike

Mike was such a good person but so many bad things happened to him. His mom was a horrible mom and eventually kicked him out of his house saying that she wasn't his mom anymore. He was only fifteen. He moved in with us and became part of our family. I will always know him as a brother. He stood up for me when I needed him and he always talked to me when I was upset. He made me feel better.

He joked around and made people laugh. He brightened people's days. I've never met anyone with such a wonderful personality even though his life was horrible.

He always seemed to be in good spirits.

One morning, my mom took me to school in our van. Mike came along for the ride because he wanted to reminisce about the school. As we pulled up to the school, he pulled down his pants and put his butt on the window. It took my mom a second to discover why I was laughing so hard. My face turned really red and my laughter made my eyes water. I gasped for breath.

My mom sped up, then hit the brakes. What happened next is something I will always remember about him. His butt slid across the window with a loud screech and he fell face first onto the van floor. The principal of the school saw it and came up to the van. He was so angry, but none of us could stop laughing. The principal was mad but couldn't do much because Mike didn't attend his school anymore.

I will never forget that moment. Mike always did spontaneous things like that and that's what made him such an unforgettable and wonderful person.

We don't talk much anymore because he moved about three hours away and has no way of getting in touch with us. I know he is doing well in his life and trying not to turn out like all his other people who have struggled.

I miss him very much and when our family gets together, I always wish he was with us. He's in my thoughts and I will never forget him.

***

As a resiliency strategy, *flow* "advances intrinsic motivation through optimal experiences as a pathway to achievement" (Conoley & Conoley, 2009).

A purposeful goal of a flow pathway is a student's well-being and happiness. While these two attributes address school engagement, the concept of *flow* more directly approaches the complementary issue of achievement (Carli, Delle, Fave, & Massimini, 1988; Mayers, 1978; Nakamura, 1988).

When a student is experiencing *flow*, he or she is deeply engaged in what some refer to as "in the groove" or "in the zone," say the Conoleys. He or she feels "cooperative in the process," awake and alert. *Flow* becomes apparent as students who are avoiding distractions absorb themselves in personally rigorous challenges ingrained in his or her capacities.

Most commonly, school-related activities or tasks involved in flow research include music, art, sports, and work. Optimal student *flow* conditions, according to the researchers, require student concentration, perceived importance to future goals (relevancy), and a healthy, strong self-esteem. Imagine flow conditions permeating within English/language arts, math, and social and natural science classrooms. Challenging activities that make use of flow research include:

- suitably challenging tasks formed around student capabilities
- attending to internal values rather than external
- an authoritative source providing communication of support
- an allowance for low structure
- tasks of high importance to the students. (Conoley & Conoley, 2009, p. 470)

Flow, as a student motivation, however, can be hampered. When external evaluations attempt to assess student performance through verbal or written judgment attempts, student *flow* conditions are at the very least threatened.

RESTRUCTURING CURRICULUM

Restructuring curriculum requires educational decision makers to become aware of not only existing organizational perceptions but those of their own as well. In many cases, these perceptions ineffectively guide program development, resulting in developmental roadblocks—obstructions leading to watered-down, informal lesson deliveries. Wheat (2009), on the other hand, looks at failing schools as being tied to low student literacy. Hiding and ignoring classroom academic struggles, he argues, can effectuate a belief that student failure is tied to some educational *natural order*.

For example, Wheat strongly encourages school and classwide conversation as a building block for increasing student literacy. When classroom conversation is inhibited, then it's easier to introduce curriculum reform but harder to make it successful. It's easier to introduce because opposition is minimal, but harder to succeed because the involvement and commitment that underlie successful change have not been fostered through discussion.

***

In failing schools, most teachers are as good as those in successful schools, Wheat tells us. The institution they work in has become dysfunctional, largely through the impact of its families and their difficult lives, and a reluctance in the school community to talk about what is going on. The curriculum is not really the problem; it's nearly always the way change is presented.

Nelson, Palonsky, and McCarthy (2007) argue that school purpose is tied to responsibilities that include determining, examining, conveying, questioning, and modifying knowledge, a responsibility at the root of issues surrounding what should be taught. As such, they suggest a flexible framing of independent knowledge control by each student. A restructuring of curriculum, therefore, might ask:

- What knowledge should we teach, in what sequence, and who gets to decide?
- Which knowledge should be required study, which should be elective, and which should be censored?
- Who should get access to which kinds of knowledge?
- How do we know if and when that or other knowledge is learned? (pp. 228–29)

Curriculum influences play a pivotal role in the quality of education received by those placed at risk of school failure, say Wang, Haertel, and Walberg (1994). The prototypical education program often contributes to student learning problems, most often through watered-down curriculum.

Wang's cohort affirms that restructuring curriculum when supported by an *inclusive, stable, supportive learning environment* can promote healthy learning for all students, comprehensive and alternative alike. Teachers help students pursue challenges while students engage the work they have chosen.

Samples of a supportive learning environment include:

- internships designed to enrich classroom learning by showing students how their learning is applied outside their school and providing students with opportunities for questioning both their academic and professional communities
- enterprises and community-based projects that produce goods and services for sale or use to people other than the students involved
- technical mentoring (or *virtual apprenticeship*) allows professionals to provide direct, systematic input to students' actual work. (Wang, Haertel, & Walberg, 1994, pp. 40–42)

Wang's learning environment requires rigorous learning objectives that not only enhance a student's choice of significant academic growth but support internships, community-based projects, and technical mentoring programs as well. And according to Lundsgaard (2004), to really understand *rigorous learning*, you have to experience it.

"When I think of rigor," Lundsgaard says, "I think of sinking my teeth into in-depth work."

Evidently, a former teacher raised a learning moment from intellectual to emotional by stretching Lundsgaard's mind to the degree that it "engaged her body and soul." It created personal challenge, a challenge that caused her to awake each morning with a burning desire to learn something new.

The rigorous part of her journey, she says, was figuring out how she was going to get where she wanted to go intellectually. "But that's what makes things fun," she said. "I did a lot of reading and independent research and worked on asking well-thought-out questions. This was self-motivated, self-directed learning that came from my personal commitment to do the very best I could for kids. It defines rigor."

Lundsgaard tells us that rigorous learning requires discovery, inquiry, and self-questioning, all parts of a rigorous whole. It's active, dominated by questioning and discovery; deep, rather than broad, project-based; and engaging, with each learner having made a connection with the material.

***

Restructuring curriculum must look at the asset-focused factor of *relevance* that speaks to "how well the values, interest, and learning priorities of the teacher are aligned with those of the students and the extent to which these aligned emphases are reflected in the curriculum," say Boykin and Noguera (2011, p. 91).

Newby (1991) found that the more a teacher invoked rewards and punishments to induce learning, the less students were engaged. He discovered that the more a teacher directly tied a lesson to familiar experiences, the more students were discernibly engaged in the lesson. He refers to the experience as *self-referencing*. His findings were not isolated: "When a question is self-referencing, students ask for it to be repeated fewer times, and are able to solve even a one-step math problem, faster" (D'Ailly, Simpson, & MacKinnon, 1997).

EFFECTIVE TEACHING APPROACHES

Gardner (2011) discusses teaching approaches that not only meet the needs of continuation school populations but offer rigorous student academic opportunities as well. He believes that the secondary years are filled with student misconceptions, stereotypes, and what he calls "rigidly applied algorithms," steps or procedures necessary to arrive at a conclusion that lack thought or understanding. He strongly suggests that high schools should be used for confronting these and other adverse cultural traits commonly held by American adolescents.

Gardner's descriptors, when applied to the needs of vulnerable student populations, can significantly increase student achievement opportunities.

He begins by suggesting that school activities confront intuitive theories, prejudices if you will, held by students at all levels. Students must adopt terminologies common to their studies then use their newly acquired language to replace previously held expressions. And when dealing with stereotypes, common in all secondary schools, Gardner recommends that students address their concerns from varying outlooks so as to allow them to address concerns from varying viewpoints.

SUMMARY

Distinguishing engagement from instructional time is evidenced when instructional time fails as compared to the engagement variable no matter the category of student engagement. The greater the interest, the greater the affective engagement.

Student affective engagement is found in student perceptions of teacher behavior. Teacher behavior is mediated by personal perceptions of students' levels of engagement as well.

Students attempting to hide from teacher interaction develop avoidance strategies that include procrastination, not trying hard, looking for excuses, avoiding help, guessing at answers, not asking questions, and working only on familiar assignments. Self-regulatory competence protects against such habits.

Four pathways leading to self-regulatory competence, an effective protective factor against avoidance, are observation, emulation, self-control, and self-regulation. Classroom engagement strongly influences these asset-focused competencies. They involve learning exchanges that build on the assets students bring into their classrooms and are encouraged by student praise, positive interactions, and anxiety-reduction exercises. Self-regulatory competence begins when students feel cared about, receive praise for their efforts, and see themselves as important to their teachers.

***

Self-determination theory holds that increased capacity generates senses of autonomy, often evidenced by students outside of alternative schools but rarely seen in their classrooms. Student self-determination shows itself when students make inferences or read between the lines during discussions—

attributes of inferential learning, an asset, by the way, most often ignored by mainstream education.

Personalized classroom instruction offers opportunities for students becoming a part of their own coursework. It conveys a sense of ownership, of relevance in a true sense. "Infusing personalization into problem texts creates an increased opportunity for students to link the problem to personal interesting information, leading to higher performance outcomes" (Boykin & Noguera, 2011). Successful personalized instruction can be seen in academic *flow*, an intrinsic motivator seen by some as "in the groove" or "in the zone."

Restructuring curriculum describes a strategy promoting healthy learning for all students. Teachers help students pursue challenges while students choose their engagements. Restructuring curriculum increases rigorous learning that offers not only discovery but also inquiry and self-questioning, all parts of a rigorous whole. It's active and deep rather than broad, and is project-based and engaging, with each learner having connected with the material.

Restructuring curriculum looks at the asset-focused factor of *relevance*, which speaks to how well the values, interest, and learning priorities of the teacher are aligned with those of the students and the extent to which these aligned emphases are reflected in the curriculum.

III

Measuring Achievement

Chapter Eight

Assessing Growth

A tiny but determined continuation school mom gently tugged on the teacher's shirt sleeve, asking, "Excuse me . . . excuse me, Senora, I have a question, please."

"Of course," the teacher replied.

"Um . . . did you say that this school is like the regular high school? I mean, do you say the credits here are as good as the ones those other kids get, you know, at the other high school?"

"Yes, of course they are. Our school is fully accredited, like our downtown feeder school, and is being recognized by the State of California as exemplary, a very high statewide honor. But, why do you ask?"

"Jaime is my youngest and he goes here. He was failing everything in the downtown school. I want him to be the first in my family to graduate. And when my older sons told Jaime and me that this was a bad school, you know . . . a school full of bad kids, they didn't want Jaime coming here. I got scared. Jaime's doing so good at this school and he's finally going to graduate soon." Tears swelled in her eyes as she commented, "I can't wait to get home and tell his older brothers what you told me. I'm so proud of Jaime. His brothers have no idea."

Assessing matters.

DOMINANT CONSORTS

According to Almeida, Le, Steinberg, & Cervantes (2010), alternative programs need flexibility. And if they are to meet requirements of the common core standards, certain ambiguities must be addressed. At one end, mandating overly rigid accountability, which leaves alternative schools without operational flexibility, needs to be readdressed. On the other hand, alternative education's complete lack of accountability fails to set appropriate expectations for alternative schools to prepare students for postsecondary success.

Almeida's team (2010) advocates that currently, states are not clear and concise enough about implementing these improvements to effectively assess the needs of alternative education.

***

Research addressing student assessment purposes fall into one of two different educational program development consorts: those who profess multiple measures, focusing mainly on the student's actual work as being a better and fairer way to evaluate student performance than standardized tests (Wolk, 2011), and those who suggest that "tests matter . . . In fact, test results tell us precisely what we need to know if we are to have any hope of refashioning instruction to bring the performance of black and Hispanic students up to the level of Asians and whites" (Thernstrom & Thernstrom, 2003, p. 4).

Both federal and state governmental support tends to be moving toward the former group in the wake of NCLB's apparent failure at meeting its rigid, self-imposed requirements.

***

"Student assessment based on multiple measures, focusing mainly on the student's actual work, is a better and fairer way to evaluate student performance than standardized tests," argues Wolk (2011). Wolk discusses Gewertz (2010) as she tells of a group of prominent educators addressing decision makers during a meeting with the National Governors Association (NGA) and the Council of Chief State School Officers (CCSSO), the main proponents of common standards and a national curriculum, along with officials from the U.S. Department of Education.

The group wants decision makers to move away from standardized multiple-choice tests, which in their opinions offer but a snapshot of student performance, to deeper, more analytical assessments and projects that require students to solve and discuss complex problems (Darling-Hammond & Haselkorn, April 1, 2009). "If assessments fail to inform instruction," adds Gene Wilhoit, the CCSSO executive director, "what good are they?"

Performance-based systems synthesize learning to instruction and evaluation to teaching, along with encouraging teachers to think deeply about levels of student performances. Additionally, performance tasks build upon relationships between teachers and students, allowing teachers to describe the standards and requirements while students are encouraged to not only select their own means of assessment but to participate in evaluating themselves as well.

"Performance-based assessments are the logical extension of personalized education. When required to be active participants in learning rather than passive receptacles of facts, students become engaged in gathering information, analyzing it, evaluating it, relating it, and applying it," Wolk professes (2011, p. 132). He argues that performance assessments have the capacity to focus on ways student work is linked to curricula and core standards.

When students do well in performance assessments, they demonstrate subject matter knowledge and, most often, a value of that awareness. Simply put, the assessment becomes in itself a form of teaching and learning.

***

Thernstrom and Thernstrom (2003) fear no nemesis as they argue assessment strengths with American educational thinkers, including Deborah Meier, cofounder of the Central Park East schools in New York; Theodore Sizer, former dean of the Harvard Graduate School of Education; and Jonathan Kozol, author of *The Shame of the Nation*, *Free Schools*, *Fire in the Ashes*, and other significant works.

These thinkers, along with an array of higher education constituents at leading graduate schools of education across the country, strongly oppose standards-based assessments in favor of alternative methods.

One of many problems, the Thernstroms contend, is that American taxpayers disagree with performance-based assessments in favor of test taking as an appropriate means of testing and evaluating student knowledge and growth levels. The researchers exemplify Public Agenda, a nonpartisan, nonprofit, widely respected public opinion research organization, who found that only 11 percent of parents thought "schools today place far too much emphasis on standardized test scores."

Seventy-one percent supported testing students at a younger age to prepare educators for a foundation in which to identify and help future strugglers. Fifty-five percent said there was "nothing wrong" with teaching to the test, since it measured important skills and knowledge. A Public Agenda poll in the winter of 1997 to 1998 found that 78 percent of black parents agreed that testing calls attention to a problem needing to be solved (Thernstrom & Thernstrom, 2003, p. 26).

***

Test-taking opponents bounce back by arguing the many limitations of test-taking assessment, not the least of which is racial bias. As the Thernstroms confront attempts by the test-taking opposition to blame racial bias on standardized tests administered throughout the country, they respond with, "How can a mathematics exam be racially biased?"

***

Stiggins and DuFour (2009) approach the argument from yet another perspective. They argue that education's current obsession with standardized testing has led to a neglect of classroom assessment that is vital to the improvement of teaching and learning, particularly the development and use of common assessments with a professional learning community structure.

Classroom assessment provides a means for teachers to synthesize their knowledge and experiences, according to the researchers, for the purposes of:

- identifying student learning needs
- improving upon instructional practices
- clarifying learning targets
- enhancing the quality of their assessments
- supporting the development of a common vision of effectiveness in teaching and learning. (pp. 164–65)

PREDICTING STUDENT STRUGGLES

Ruiz de Velasco and McLaughlin (2012) report that most often, continuation teachers reveal a need to identify early warning signals of student classroom performance struggles. They report that teachers want to know how to work with diverse learners. They look forward to organizing classrooms and managing practices specific to their instructional goals and objectives. Building trust with students, according to the interviewers, is not only central for these teachers but also necessary in predicting their students' academic, social, and emotional struggles.

Stiggins and DuFour conclude that assessments expose predictors of oncoming student throes and support rigorous achievement.

***

Balfanz, Bridgeland, Bruce, & Hornig-Fox (2012) tell us that the highest predictors of approaching student performance struggles include absenteeism, schoolwide misbehavior, and struggling course performance. Twenty or more missed school days along with an absentee rate of 10 percent or more during a given school year defines an early predictor, they argue.

Two or more mild or more serious behavior infractions alert stakeholders to future classroom performance struggles, say the study team. And evidence of a student's inability to read at grade level by the end of third grade; failure in English or math in sixth through ninth grades; GPA of less than 2.0; two or more failures in ninth grade; and failure to earn on-time promotion to tenth grade are all predictors of not only student classroom performance struggles but dropping out of school altogether.

Detecting early warning signals provided by struggling student performances grew from a powerful idea into a research-based reform area of study. A lack of available data provided by an Early Warning Indicator and Intervention System (EWS) has resulted in educational stakeholders missing early intervention opportunities. The Balfanz cohort reports that:

> The 2011 Civic Enterprises/Everyone Graduates Center report, *On Track for Success: The Use of Early Warning Indicator and Intervention Systems to Build a Grad Nation*, represents the first national assessment of EWS at the district, state and national levels. The report shares evidence from the latest research and best practices, examining detailed progress being made in 16 districts and communities, and in seven states. It also offers a comprehensive definition of EWS as a collaborative approach among stakeholders to using data effectively to keep students on a pathway to graduation. (p. 42)

Balfanz et al. (2012) tell us that a combination of features characterizing the best EWS include: a rapid identification of troubled students; immediate interventions targeted to student needs; frequent intervention assessments; and immediate modifications of struggling interventions and shared findings.

ASSESSING STUDENT PERFORMANCE

The two dominant consorts pushing and pulling one another at the expense of purposeful student growth fail to realize the value each bring to the table. Testing is a fact of everyday living from taking driver's tests to preparing for a state bar exam. Students from all walks of life prepare for entry-level aptitude and placement tests required by career-level employers, SAT and ACT college-level entrance exams, and never-ending testing occurring throughout higher education and job advancement.

Testing is not going away, and students must be aptly prepared, a responsibility of any effective high school, continuation or otherwise.

Multiple measurements not only allow for immediate feedback evidencing student capacity levels, they enrich the depth and breadth of learning by encouraging a student to dig deeper into a subject, if for no other reason than personal satisfaction. It is a foundation, a bedrock, if you will, for personalizing student curriculum design, keeping pace with individual growth, and measuring results. Both consorts, testing and multiple measurement, provide formative and summative assessment opportunities that not only identify student interest but also drive curriculum and measure outcome.

***

Professional organizations are well equipped to provide test-taking preparation manuals and/or seminars for academic communities. Preparation books are offered by bookstores for an array of student and professional requirements. Most state educational testing requirements provide test preparation material as well. And clearly identified, goal-directed classroom lessons can be readily assessed through testing and multiple measurement strategies that applied together can provide effective student learning exercises as well as capacity awareness.

DEMONSTRATING ASSESSMENT TOOLS AND STRATEGIES

As students work in small groups trying to determine Martin Luther King's purpose in his 1968 *Letter from a Birmingham Jail*, they argue rhetoric they believe particularly effective, then analyze how its effectiveness contributes to the letter's persuasiveness (CCSS Reading for Informational Text 6-12: 6). Each assessment is personally chosen, then successfully defended by each student to their teacher.

One student prepares a written test designed to assess the quality of learning class members will obtain from an activity designed by her. Another prepares a rubric allowing class members to score performance levels of debate participants who will be arguing the effectiveness of the selected rhetoric.

Still another will write a five-hundred-to-one-thousand-word paper detailing the outcomes of both assessment strategies, then present it to the class, inviting arguments that will be measured on an instrument designed during the presentation of the first two assessments by the teacher. The teacher, rather than her students, will provide evidence of the outcome. The final step, however, requires the outcome to receive a majority approval by the class, and if not, the class will override the teacher and provide the final determination of the outcome. Assessments provide powerful learning opportunities.

SUMMARY

Two very different assessment designs fall into one of two program development consorts: those believing in multiple measures, focusing on student work, and those supporting student performances on standardized tests.

Performance-based systems synthesize learning to instruction and evaluation to teaching while encouraging teachers to think deeply about levels of student performances. Performance tasks build upon relationships between teachers and students while students are encouraged to not only select their own assessment measures but to participate in their personal evaluation processes as well. Simply put, the assessment becomes, in itself, a form of teaching and learning.

The American taxpayers disagree with performance-based assessments, say the Thernstroms (2003), who argue that 89 percent of parents support testing as an appropriate means of determining academic growth and ability. Stiggins and DeFour (2009) continue the discussion by including their belief that education's current obsession with standardized testing has led to a neglect of classroom assessment.

Balfanz, Bridgeland, Bruce, & Hornig-Fox (2012) tell us that schools need to look at assessments from yet another viewpoint, one that predicts approaching student performance struggles from early ages such as absenteeism, schoolwide misbehavior, and struggling course performances. They argue that assessment energies are being misdirected and should identify student adversities every bit as much as academic performances.

Student participation in relevant assessments provide powerful learning opportunities, especially when their efforts result in decisive outcomes.

Chapter Nine

Laquitta and Jonathan

Experience has shown that adolescents with adverse histories react strongly and immediately to responsible faculties and stakeholders who demonstrate care and concern for not only their school successes but also their persons—their overall well-beings.

Staff members show concern for their students, and discover wants and needs conducive to helping students launch their curricula. For example, through personal conversations, essays, debates, assignment responses, and other communicative resources, caring teachers become aware of student concerns, interests, ambitions, and dreams. Student/teacher interactions allow for an awareness of student intelligences, which most often pair with prominent learning styles.

These data, synthesized with student resiliencies generating strong senses of personal self-efficacies, offer unlimited opportunities for strong, rigorous learning.

***

Further experience has shown that watered-down learning criteria receive strong dissatisfaction from resilient continuation students who voice their concerns promptly and with doubtless intent. At the same time, purposeful students demand an answer to *why* —why do I need to know the material?

As answers are accepted by continuation students who are assured that their teachers have their backs, barriers to their educational achievements give way. Answers, however, must be real. They must be relevant to each student's wants and needs and be rigorous by all standardized measurements, including a state's college preparatory requirements, common core standard levels, and most importantly, levels of student demands for academic and personal respect.

***

Taxpayers, along with increasing numbers of secondary stakeholders, are asking why students who come to school hungry would concern themselves with algebra, geometry, or any higher-level mathematics? How might a common core social studies curriculum offset the day-to-day tensions absorbing a homeless student? Will college prep science courses provide students with acceptable, at least neat and clean, school clothing?

If, as some suggest, it is not a school's responsibility to clothe, feed, and house students, impoverished or otherwise, how then can schools break through these barriers so they can not only allow student learning, but improve it as well?

Synthesizing personal student concerns with learning levels offered by college prep and common core standards can overcome any illusion that rigorous academic achievement is irrelevant to *real-world* concerns. Achievement in the academic, standards-based learning arena offers solutions, theoretical as well as practical, at all student concern levels. Schools must simply design and develop effective pedagogies that synthesize student viewpoints with not only their own but those required by their states as well.

This idea offers remarkable possibilities. A homeless student, for example, can improve his or her living conditions by first understanding, then using "stated assumptions, definitions, and previously established results in constructing arguments," a Common Core State Standard (CCSS) for mathematical practice. This standard builds conceptual understanding that is well suited for teaching students to overcome a lifetime of economic adversity.

Furthermore, students who have learned to evaluate and assess the credibility of informational sources including primary and secondary sources along with Internet sources and the media (Los Angeles County Office of Education: CCSS, History/Social Studies, 2011) will develop capacities to provide healthy and nutritious meals for themselves and their families on a long-term, permanent basis.

These claims, however, are not the intended products of the CCSS initiative. They simply provide a key, if you will, for unlocking doors that hide rigorous, proficient educational opportunities for alternative students who have been thus far denied.

A beginning step at designing effective common core pedagogy for our nation's most vulnerable high-schoolers is to build upon their senses of self-efficacy. As they realize the relationships between their personal concerns and common core achievement, fresh, new opportunities await them as their learning reaches the intended goals and objectives of common core designers. Laquitta and Jonathan provide the evidence.

***

She was going to hurt somebody . . . really.

Mr. Ramos had seen her like this before. Her jawline defines itself by tightening the muscular patterns produced by her clenched teeth.

Mr. Ramos sat down beside her and waited a few moments before quietly whispering how much he enjoyed having her in class. Her last essay comparing the merits of a Jack London story with those belonging to several Charles Dickens pieces were fresh and appealing. Most importantly, they were convincing. She's developing an understanding, even an appreciation. "I know you hurt," he said. "Can I help?" Laquitta glanced around to see if anyone in the class was watching.

"It's my mother. I hate her. She's always taking her boyfriend's side over mine. She doesn't trust me; she never did." Throwing her hands up, Laquitta whispered at voice level, "Why? I didn't do anything to her, Mr. Ramos. Why's she always putting me down in front of everyone? Now she's put me on punishment cuz I came home late last night. She knew I was with Jeremy. I'm always with Jeremy. She loves Jeremy!"

"How old are you, Laquitta?" She knew Mr. Ramos already knew.

"Seventeen."

"And how old did you tell me your mom was when she had you?" He was careful.

"Fifteen and a half," she responded. "But I'm not my mom! She doesn't have to think because she was her way, I will be too. I hate her. I hate her!"

"Do me a favor," he asked. "Walk over to Denny's and get a hamburger. It's almost lunchtime anyway. You'll still get the hour. Relax and get your mind off your drama. See me during my sixth period prep. I think I can help."

"Okay, but I swear to God, Mr. Ramos. I'm not putting up with her crap anymore. I'm just not!"

"I'll see you sixth period, Laquitta. Here's a couple of bucks. Let me cover the hamburger."

"Thanks," Laquitta replied, hanging her head low. She wondered if Mr. Ramos knew she had no lunch money. She rarely did.

In sixth period, Mr. Ramos was correcting essay conventions as Laquitta strolled into the classroom. She had a little more spring in her step than earlier. He first thought maybe hunger played a role in her earlier outbursts, but he knew of Laquitta's struggle with her mom. It seemed to be an ongoing, relational conflict. She sat opposite his desk and remained quiet.

"I need your help, Laquitta," he commented, "but I need you wanting to help, rather than being assigned to help . . . know what I mean?"

She nodded and he continued, "Whenever you call your mom, 'Mother,' you show how much you not only love her, but respect her. We've talked about this before." Again she nodded. "I've been getting a lot of essays lately that show a lot of others share your problem. Looking at your work these past few months, I think you may be able to help some of the students in your class better than I can."

Laquitta listened.

Mr. Ramos asked her to remove herself from her emotional attachment to her mom for a couple of weeks. Laquitta needed to learn her mom's thoughts and beliefs regarding her family and what she needed to do to live with them. Her mom became her study assignment.

Laquitta would carry a small spiral notebook with her so she could record her mom's behaviors while interacting with her family members and responsibilities throughout each day. That's all. Others could only be convinced of Laquitta's conclusions if she did not interfere in her mom's actions in any way, at least in the beginning. Her study also required her to completely obey her mother's restrictions without argument. If confronted by her mom, she was to avoid any and all dispute. She had to respond to her mom in a noncombative, yet credible manner.

Laquitta had gathered data before, primarily from newspaper articles, TV commentaries, websites, literary sources, interviews, and observational notes. But she had never attempted to observe someone close to her. She wasn't sure she could.

Three rather than two weeks later, Laquitta asked a classmate to help her identify data from her notes, then categorize them. If disagreement could not be amended, Laquitta would invite another student to help satisfy the process. Other than blaming her mom for being passed out on the sofa due to a lacking evidence of alcohol, there was no help needed in identifying data.

The girls agreed that the evidence fell into three categories: mom's concerns for her children's health, safety, and future living conditions. Laquitta gathered substantial evidence of her mom borrowing, bumming, and sneaking money from whomever and whatever sources available to her. Her mother's uncompromising fear of her kids going hungry developed an addictive behavior of stashing every dime she could for grocery money, money she knew she would need at some later, unforeseen date.

Laquitta witnessed her mom exploding emotionally over not only Laquitta's late evening endeavors but behavioral choices made by her younger brothers and sister as well. The more Laquitta and her classmate Kristi studied the categories, the deeper Laquitta's understanding of her mother's familial fears and concerns became. Laquitta was demoralized by her former, hateful feelings. She decided to test her assumptions.

"Mom, you're so right about me being inconsiderate when I stay out all night with Jeremy, or anyone else for that matter. With your permission, I'd like to go over to Jeremy's tonight and hang out. If it's okay, I'll call and let you know what's going on and where we'll be. I'll be home no later than midnight and you can trust that. We just fall asleep anyway."

"If you need me to look after the kids cuz you have something going on, Jeremy can come over here . . . again, if that's okay with you. We just won't go out. We can always go out some other time anyway. Yea?"

Laquitta's mom was stunned. She cautiously asked, "Are you feeling okay, young lady? I mean, you've never even suggested something like this before. What's going on?"

"I dunno, Ma. I'm just tired of me being all about me, ya know? I got to thinking about what you got to do all the time and about how much I add to it. I dunno. Anyway . . . "

"I can't believe what you are saying, Laquitta. Are you growing up on me? No. You go out with Jeremy tonight. You have a good time. I don't have any plans, go ahead. Call me when you're ready to come home so I don't worry. Really. Go. Have a good time."

Laquitta continued testing her assumptions.

Every hour or so, she called her mom to see if she needed anything and to tell her she was fine. She'd see her later on, earlier than normal, sometime around 11:00. Laquitta was tired, anyway, but not too tired to stop taking notes. She now recorded her own behaviors and compared their results to her mother's behavior before her own, personal intervening. The differences were more than remarkable, they were stunning. Laquitta was ready for her presentation.

***

The classroom announcement board gave ample notice of Laquitta's presentation on a Wednesday, fourth period, right after advising. Students were notified that the period was reserved for a student presentation, thereby setting aside any other student study. Credit points were offered for participation. As the room settled down, Mr. Ramos stood up and prepared the class by first describing the reasons for the presentation followed by student participation rules. He then introduced Laquitta to a loud, enthusiastic applause.

The room was packed. Laquitta slowly rose to stand in front of her class. She wore a slightly embarrassed smile while carrying a two-page set of notes she used for a safety net. Laquitta knew she would not refer to them.

She began by looking straight at a group of her closest friends and firmly asking, "You remember about a month ago when my mom put me on restriction simply for the fact I was over at Jeremy's and fell asleep . . . huh? You remember how she was always hating on me, expecting me to do her job instead of her? Remember how she hung out with her boyfriend and stuck me with my brothers and sister all the time?" She cocked her head to the side and threw up her arms with her hands bent at the wrists, "What was that all about, you know? When was I going to get to be a teenager? What about me?"

"Yeeeah!" the class yelled out. A loud roar of agreement followed with everyone trying to outdo one another with their own stories, too confusing and mixed to understand. Laquitta let it burn itself out before continuing. "Mr. Ramos felt my struggle, so he asked if he could help. When I told him what happened, he said that a bunch of you had similar problems and that I should do this assignment. So here I am."

"Look," Laquitta began, "Fixin' my life means fixin' me . . . know what I mean? I mean, I finally learned that."

"See, Mr. Ramos had me separate myself from my anger by watching my mom around the house and taking notes on how she acts. Kristi and I got together and organized the stuff we found in the notes; you know, categorized them. First we had to take out the things my mom did, then you know, put them in like either *children's health*, *safety*, or *future living conditions*. By doing this, Kristi and I saw that my mom got pissed off mostly because she was worried that there wouldn't be enough food in the house or that when I stayed out all night, I might be ganging up or getting pregnant."

Laquitta dropped her head slightly. "She worries about what'll happen if we get evicted next month or where we'll end up when we're grown. My mom worries a lot, mostly about her family . . . you know, all of us . . . yea."

She continued, "When I learned all this, it hit me that my mom isn't a hater. She don't hate me . . . know what I mean? It's like, you know, she takes care of us all by herself, you know? She has that nasty job over at the motel where they don't even give her enough hours so she has to work over at McDonald's, too. Then she has to come home to my crap? I mean . . . sorry, Mr. Ramos . . . to me and my brothers' and sister's stuff? I'm just sayin' . . ."

Laquitta shuffled her feet while looking down, "She needs and deserves some help, man. It's like, I gotta 'man-up' here . . . or maybe 'woman-up.' Whatever."

The classroom was dead quiet.

"So I, uh, huh," Laquitta wiped away her beginning tears, "I started cleaning up the house. And if my little brothers and sister don't help, I beat 'em down. I don't care what my momma says, if they live here, they gonna keep this place clean and do their part with school work and their chores. That's right, they gonna get chores and I'll make sure they do 'em. Why should my momma have to do everything, know what I mean?"

Laquitta was on a roll. "I also got a job over at Taco Bell. They let me take home food they don't sell by the end of the night and I use most of my paychecks for the other food my family needs. Why should my mom worry about all of us being hungry? When I get some more hours, I'll have enough to replace all our nasty clothes too. My brothers and sister are gonna be dipped in butter, no matter what."

She didn't have to push it any further. Everyone understood. She lowered her head, wiped away her tears, and looked brazenly out to her audience, "It ain't your mom or your people. It ain't Mr. Ramos or your teachers here. It ain't even your boss at work for some of you with jobs," she learned.

"It's *you*, man. It always was. It's always gonna be."

"You gotta get you right so you can be there for others, you know, others who count. And who knows, maybe even for others who don't count, I dunno. I'm just sayin' that my mom respects me now. I mean, she talks *with me* now instead of *at me*." Laquitta straightened upright. "She thanks me a lot for my help with the house and the food and the way my kid brothers and sister act. And I thank her for being my mom and for all she does for us when she doesn't really have to."

She slowly scanned her audience.

"I mean we all know a lot of kids livin' in foster homes, right? It's just that, she's always there for us. She's got our backs. And I gotta tell ya, I wonder how many of your moms out there got your backs too, huh? And what are you doin' about it? That's all I got to say." Laquitta quietly took her seat. The room remained quiet. No one said a word. Then it exploded.

Students applauded, whistled, and stood up, screaming for Laquitta to acknowledge them. She stood up once again, thanked them, then tried to sit down as students kept yelling questions at her. She calmed them down, and they took their seats. She looked out at them and with a quiet grin, simply asked, "Questions?"

Laquitta spent the next fifteen minutes responding to questions thrown at her by her class. Some wanted to know how she got her job at Taco Bell, while others asked how she kept her siblings in line. Some wanted to know if she had time to hang out with her friends, while others wished their moms were as cool as Laquitta's. Most wanted to know how she was able to do what she did.

She told them that she discovered a connection between what her school was teaching and her own life. She found out that when asked to "determine the meaning of words as they are used in a text so that she can analyze how an author refines the key terms" or "to integrate and evaluate multiple sources of information presented in different formats to solve a problem," she was applying civic learning to current issues in today's society, including the societal conditions of her own family and neighborhood.

She simply needed to learn what the words meant. No big deal. She first Googled them, then rewrote the sentences using her own words for meaning so she could reread the sentences to learn how the vocabulary worked. It was a little time consuming, but as Laquitta would say, "Look at me and my mom!"

"My neighborhood has a language all its own, you know? So does yours," Laquitta informed the class. "Listen to your moms, sometimes. They even have their own language. Everyone does, even schools and their books. The thing is, school language, or as Mr. Ramos calls it, 'appropriate conversational usage,' gets you things nothing else does. It doesn't just get you credit points or diplomas. Oh, it will if that's all you want. But it'll also show you how to understand, appreciate, build some skills, problem-solve, and more. It'll even show you how anything you want can be had by what you learn in school, even more."

"I mean, I used to hang out at malls and liquor stores because all my friends did. Now I hang out in classrooms and the library. I looked around. Where do you find people who have what you want . . . liquor stores? Yea, right. Look, we all spend our time one way or the other. I find people who have what I want hanging around schools and colleges with their faces shoved in books. I know a lot of you say, 'Whatever,' but I'm just saying, 'Fixin' my life means fixin' me.' And the same's true for all of you."

***

It's not what we do in our classrooms that matter. It's what our students do. Standards printed in the upper corners of high school textbooks do not determine the value of a lesson or the elevation of its rigor. How a student behaves during and after the lesson does. It's about students. Programs and their lessons simply provide the pathways for student growth. They provide a means for elevating students to academic capacities that prepare them for college and career level readiness. Yet for some reason, teachers mostly address what they're doing in their classrooms rather than what their students are doing.

Sometimes, however, a student success bends a truth, rarely if ever found in a teacher's intent. One such student, Jonathan, was working with the first standard from the pink packets, *Reading Standards for Informational Text*. The lesson wanted him to learn how to: Cite strong and thorough textual evidence to support analysis of what the text says explicitly as well as inferences drawn from the text, including determining where the text leaves matters uncertain (CCSS Reading 11-12 Informational Text, 1).

Jonathan stood third in line, waiting for his English class to open up for first period. He had to get here early in order to make sure he got a seat. He stayed up half the night first reviewing, then studying, A. E. Houseman's, "When I Was One and Twenty," a short poem attempting to reason why romance perpetuates pain in a relationship. Kristi broke up with him Thursday, and he's working hard to make sense out of his pain. It's his way of pushing his hurt aside.

Anyway, he's not sure that's possible, so he looked to literature for answers. It's worked for him before. Along with other issues, Houseman tries to convince his readers that romantic love has no choice but to conclude painfully. Jonathan can't figure out why feeling so good back when Kristi and he were talking could hurt so badly when they break up. Where'd the pain come from? He didn't hurt before he met Kristi, so why is he hurting so much now?

Jonathan argues that the color of the language effectuated by Houseman's word usage exposes the author's recent, very personal love loss. Houseman's trying to describe lessons others tried to teach him but he refused to learn.

How come nobody tried to teach *him* anything before he started talking to Kristi?

Romantic love coming apart, according to Jonathan's analysis of Houseman's work, has to be experienced. It can't be taught. But Jonathan doesn't believe that. And he doesn't know why. He keeps trying to find other context hidden among and between the lines, but he can't avoid Houseman's painful message informing his readers that love hurts . . . period.

Jonathan set the poem down, stared out the classroom window, and failed to discover the source of his pain. He concluded that it's not Kristi's nor his fault. It's love's fault. Fall in love . . . feel the pain. That's what Houseman argues.

Still . . . he wonders.

Jonathan, unsatisfied, pulled up a chair alongside Mr. Ramos's desk. Mr. Ramos listened carefully before asking the class for a ten-minute debate, an interrupting class activity designed to support a student's project assessment. Classes are always asked permission for any interruption, and students jump at the opportunity. Not only are their opinions respected, the debate often shines light on their own personal concerns, project-based or otherwise.

It's not really a formal debate anyway. That's just what Mr. Ramos calls it. And it's never allowed beyond ten minutes; otherwise, the debates would take time from everyone else's work.

***

Jonathan presented his concerns to his classmates, who listened quietly and attentively. His moist eyes demonstrated the gravity of his struggles.

The class embraced his level of trust in them, and they thought quietly before debating his conclusions. His teacher remained quiet, a requirement of a ten-minute debate session, unless of course, disruption occurs. Rachael, sitting toward the back of the room, commented while raising her hand, "Jonathan, Houseman doesn't tell you why, only *that* love hurts. Others didn't tell him why, only *that* . See what I mean? You want him to tell you *why* . I say he can't do that because he doesn't know. He hurts, himself, y'know? He's all about *that* , not *why* ."

"I dunno, Rachael. Jonathan may be asking other questions, questions that wonder why love at all?" said Chaday. "If pain is really a requirement of love, why love? Love is supposed to be a foundation of human purpose, but how can it be if pain is a requirement?"

Chaday continued. "I hear what Rachael's saying about Jonathan rethinking his feelings for his ex, but can feelings really be rethought? I mean, I suppose they can, but so what? Feelings are, by their very nature, meant to be felt. You have to feel them. When they hurt, they hurt, and when they love, they feel good! C'mon, that's why we talk to guys and guys talk to us. We love the feelings! And feelings require trust, which in turn identifies the risk of loving, yea?" She wasn't asking as much as informing.

"When we trust love's help and support, then discover we can't trust someone we love, the impact of that discovery attacks the love, leaving us lost and afraid," Chaday argued. "That's the source of your pain. I should know. Randy cheated on me and I hate him! You can't trust any a' those dudes. Who needs 'em!"

Jonathan slowly looked up, eyes red but dry. He didn't hear a word Chaday said. He kept thinking, "Rachael's hot. I wonder if she'd go out with me."

Sometimes the Common Core goes places their designers didn't anticipate.

***

Laquitta and Jonathan interacted with two rigorous eleventh- and twelfth-grade Common Core English/Language Arts standards: Speaking & Listening 11-12, (4a) and Reading Informational Text 11-12, (1). Both students not only introduced their standard to their struggles, they learned to cite strong evidence and analyze its development over the course of their concerns.

Both were able to analyze the impact of a presenter's choices regarding how to develop and relate elements of a story or drama to meet its purpose and to present supporting evidence conveying a clear and distinct perspective and argument such that listeners can follow the line of reasoning in a style appropriate to purpose, audience, and a range of formal and informal tasks. As students realize that James Baldwin, Jack London, Langston Hughes, and a seemingly infinite number of other writers provide them with equally powerful problem-solving capacities, they use what they learned to reach out. Sometimes, they even grab.

So do you, and so do I.

When we experience rich, wonderful feelings from embracing a passage found in a significant piece of literature, we learn. And we solve problems directly and indirectly with and from that learning. So do our students.

What we do in classes matters mostly when it directly leads to assessable student learning. The results of our teaching are shown by what our students do. Assessments matter. Assessment-focused lessons drive achievement. Knowing where our students are going and what it will look like when they get there embraces our program and classwork development. Our kids deserve the benefits of the outcomes.

References

Adler, M. (1927). *Dialectic.* New York: Harcourt Brace.
Allen, V. (1976). The helping relationship and socialization of children: Some perspectives on tutoring. In J. L. Nelson, S. B. Palonsky, & M. R. McCarthy, *Critical issues in education.* 6th ed. Boston: McGraw Hill, 2007, p. 8.
Almeida, C., Le, C., Steinberg, A., and Cervantes, R. (2010 September). Reinventing alternative education: An assessment of current state policy and how to improve it. *Jobs for the Future.*
Anand, P. G., and Ross, S. M. (1987). Using computer-assisted instruction to personalize arithmetic materials for elementary school children. *Journal of Educational Psychology* 79, no. 1, 72–78. In A. W. Boykin and P. Noguera, *Creating the opportunity to learn: Moving from research to practice to close the achievement gap.* Alexandria, VA: ASCD, 2011, pp. 93–95.
Aronson, J., Fried, C., and Good, C. (2002). Reducing the effects of stereotype threat on African American college students by shaping theories of intelligence. *Journal of Experimental Social Psychology* 38, no. 2, 113–25. In A. W. Boykin and P. Noguera, *Creating the opportunity to learn: Moving from research to practice to close the achievement gap.* Alexandria, VA: ASCD, 2011, p. 62.
Balfanz, R., Bridgeland, J. M., Bruce, M., Hornig-Fox, J. (2012). *Building a grad nation: Progress and challenge in ending the high school dropout epidemic.* Manuscript submitted for publication, Civic Enterprises: Everyone Graduates Center at Johns Hopkins University: America's Promise Alliance; Alliance for Excellent Education.
Bamburg, J. (1994). *Raising expectations to improve student learning.* Naperville, IL: North Central Regional Educational Laboratory, Learning Point Associates. In C. B. Dean and D. Parsley, Changing schools: Re-imagine high performance. *Success in Sight Module 4: School Culture & Change: Leveraging the Power of Productive Mindsets,* 2006.
Bandura, A. (1994). Self-efficacy. In *Encyclopedia of human behavior,* volume 4, edited by V. S. Ramachandran, pp. 71–81. In A. W. Boykin and P. Noguera, *Creating the opportunity to learn: Moving from research to practice to close the achievement gap.* Alexandria, VA: ASCD, 2011, pp. 54–55.
Bandura, A. (1997). *Self-efficacy: The exercise of control.* New York: W. H. Freeman.
Blackwell, L. A., Trzesniewski, K. H., and Dweck, C. S. (2007). Implicit theories of intelligence predict achievement across an adolescent transition: A longitudinal study and an intervention. *Child Development* 78, no. 1, 246–63. In A. W. Boykin and P. Noguera, *Creating the opportunity to learn: Moving from research to practice to close the achievement gap.* Alexandria, VA: ASCD, 2011.

Blumenfeld-Jones, D. (2004). The hope of a critical ethics. *Educational Theory* 54, no. 3: 263–79. In J. L. Nelson, S. B. Palonsky, & M. R. McCarthy, *Critical issues in education*. 6th ed. Boston: McGraw Hill, 2007, p. 8.

Bodovski, K. J., and Farkas, G. (2007). Mathematics growth in early elementary school: The roles of beginning knowledge, student engagement, and instruction. *Elementary School Journal* 108, no. 2, 116–30. In A. W. Boykin and P. Noguera, *Creating the opportunity to learn: Moving from research to practice to close the achievement gap*. Alexandria, VA: ASCD, 2011.

Boykin, A. W., and Noguera, P. (2011). *Creating the opportunity to learn: Moving from research to practice to close the achievement gap*. Alexandria, VA: ASCD.

Bridgeland, J. M., Dilulio, J. J., and Burke-Morison, K. (2006, March). The silent epidemic: Perspectives of high school dropouts. https://docs.gatesfoundation.org/documents/thesilentepidemic3-06final.pdf.

Brookover, W. B., and Lezotte, L. W. (1979). *Changes in school characteristics coincident with changes in student achievement*. East Lansing, MI: Michigan State University College of Urban Development. In M. M. Kirby and M. F. DiPaola, *Academic optimism and achievement: A path model*. In W. K. Hoy & M. F. DiPaola, *Studies in school improvement*. Charlotte: Information Age Publishing, 2009.

Bryk, A. S., Lee, V. E., and Holland, P. B. (1993). *Catholic schools and the common good*. Cambridge, MA: Harvard University Press.

Carli, M., Fave, A. D., and Massimini, F. (1988). The quality of experience in the flow channels: Comparison of Italian and U.S. students. In Csikszentmihalyi & Csikszentmihalyi, eds., 1988, pp. 288–318.

Casteel, C. (1997). Attitudes of African American and Caucasian eighth grade students about praises, rewards and punishments. *Elementary School Guidance and Counseling* 31, no. 4, 262–72. In A. W. Boykin and P. Noguera, *Creating the opportunity to learn: Moving from research to practice to close the achievement gap*. Alexandria, VA: ASCD, 2011, p. 76.

CDE. (2010). California Department of Education. A report to the legislature and Governor Pursuant to Chapter 681, Statues of 2008. *Multiple Pathways to Student Success: Envisioning the New California High School*. Sacramento, CA. http://www.schoolsmovingup.net.

Center for Disease Control and Prevention, Adolescent Health. (2007). *Protective factors and school connectedness*.

Chan, L. K. S., and Moore, P. J. (2006). Development of attributional beliefs and strategic knowledge in years 5–9: A longitudinal analysis. *Educational Psychology* 26, no. 2: 161–85.

Character Education Partnerships (n.d.). *Developing and assessing school culture: A new level of accountability for schools*. http://www.rucharacter.org/file/DevelopingandAssessingSchoolCulture_Final%5B1%5D.pdf.

Chirkov, V. I., Ryan, R. M., Kim, Y., and Kaplan, U. (2003). Differentiating autonomy from individualism and independence: A self-determination theory perspective on internalization of cultural orientations and well-being. *Journal of Personality and Social Psychology* 84, no. 1, 97–110. In A. W. Boykin and P. Noguera, *Creating the opportunity to learn: Moving from research to practice to close the achievement gap*. Alexandria, VA: ASCD, 2011, p. 85.

Comber, B., and Simpson, A., eds. (2001). *Negotiating critical literacies in classrooms*. Mahwah, NJ: Erlbaum. In J. L. Nelson, S. B. Palonsky, & M. R. McCarthy, *Critical issues in education*. 6th ed. Boston: McGraw Hill, 2007, p. 227.

Conoley, C. W., and Conoley, J. C. (2009). *Positive psychology for educators*. In Gilman, Huebner, & Furlong, eds., 2009.

Cooper, D., ed. (1967). *To free a generation: The dialectics of liberalism*. New York: Collier. In J. L. Nelson, S. B. Palonsky, & M. R. McCarthy, *Critical issues in education*. 6th ed. Boston: McGraw Hill, 2007, p. 8.

Cordova, D. I., and Lepper, M. R. (1996). Intrinsic motivation and the process of learning: Beneficial effects of contextualization, personalization, and choice. *Journal of Educational Psychology* 99, no. 4, 715–30. In A. W. Boykin and P. Noguera, *Creating the opportunity to learn: Moving from research to practice to close the achievement gap*. Alexandria, VA: ASCD, 2011, p. 96.

Csikszentmihalyi, M. (1997). *Finding flow.* New York: Basic Books. In Gilman, Huebner, and Furlong, 2009, p. 470.

D'Ailly, H. H., Simpson, J., and MacKinnon, G. E. (1997). Where should "you" go in a math compare problem? *Journal of Educational Psychology* 89, no. 3, 562–67. In A. W. Boykin & P. Noguera, *Creating the opportunity to learn: Moving from research to practice to close the achievement gap.* Alexandria, VA: ASCD, 2011, p. 93.

Dallmann-Jones, A. (2006). *Shadow children: Understanding education's #1 problem.* Lancaster, PA: RLD Publications, Inc.

Darling-Hammond, L., and Haselkorn, D. (2009, April 1). Reforming teaching: Are we missing the boat? *Education Week* 28, no. 27, 30, 36. http://www.edweek.org/ew/articles/2009/04/01/27hammond.h28.html.

Dean, C., and Parsley, D. (2011). Changing schools: Re-imagine high performance. *Success in Sight Module 4: School Culture & Change: Leveraging the Power of Productive Mindsets.* http://www.mcrel.org/success-in-sight.

Delpit, L. (1988). The silenced dialogue: Power and pedagogy in educating other people's children. *Harvard Educational Review* 58, no. 3, 280–98. In A. W. Boykin and P. Noguera, *Creating the opportunity to learn: Moving from research to practice to close the achievement gap.* Alexandria, VA: ASCD, 2011, pp. 110–11.

Dianda, M. R. (2008). *Preventing future high school dropouts: An advocacy and action guide for NEA state and local affiliates.* National Education Association (NEA). Washington, DC. Human and Civil Rights. http://www.nea.org/assets/docs/HE/dropoutguide1108.pdf.

Dryfoos, J. G. (1994). *Full-service schools: A revolution in health and social service for children, youth and families.* San Francisco: Jossey-Bass. In W. H. Parrett and K. M. Budge, *Turning high-poverty schools into high-performing schools.* Alexandria, Virginia: ASCD, 2012, p. 127.

Dryfoos, J. G., and Maguire, S. (2002). *Inside full-service community schools.* Thousand Oaks, CA: Corwin. In W. H. Parrett and K. M. Budge, *Turning high-poverty schools into high-performing schools.* Alexandria, Virginia: ASCD, 2012, p. 127.

Dweck, C. S. (1999). *Self-theories: Their role in motivation, personality, and development.* Philadelphia: Psychology Press.

Dweck, C. S., and Leggett, E. L. (1988). A social-cognitive approach to motivation and personality. *Psychology Review* 95, no. 2, 256–73. In W. Boykin and P. Noguera, *Creating the opportunity to learn: Moving from research to practice to close the achievement gap.* Alexandria, VA: ASCD, 2011.

Edmonds, R. R. (1979). Some schools work and more can. *Social Policy* 10, 28–32. In M. M. Kirby and M. F. DiPaola, *Academic optimism and achievement: A path model*, in W. K. Hoy & M. F. DiPaola, *Studies in school improvement.* Charlotte: Information Age Publishing, 2009.

Edmonds, R. R. (1981). Making public schools effective. *Social Policy* 10, 56–60.

EdSource (May 2008). California's continuation schools. *EdSource Research Summary.*

Ellis, A., and Harper, R. A. (1997). *A guide to rational living.* Chatsworth, CA: Wilshire Book Company.

Erbe, B. M. (2000). Correlates of school achievement in Chicago elementary schools. Chicago: Roosevelt University, Department of Education. In M. M. Kirby and M. F. DiPaola, *Academic optimism and achievement: A path model.* In W. K. Hoy & M. F. DiPaola, *Studies in school improvement.* Charlotte: Information Age Publishing, 2009.

Farrar, R. C. (2000). *Sartrean dialectics.* Lanham, MD: Lexington Books.

Fredericks, J. A., Blumenfeld, P. C., and Paris, A. H. (2004). School engagement: Potential of the concept, state of evidence. *Review of Educational Research* 74, no. 1, 59–109. In A. W. Boykin and P. Noguera, *Creating the opportunity to learn: Moving from research to practice to close the achievement gap.* Alexandria, VA: ASCD, 2011.

Freire, P. (1970). *Pedagogy of the oppressed.* New York, London: Continuum International Publishing Group.

Freire, P., and Macedo, D. (1987). *Literacy.* South Hadley, MA: Bergin & Garvey. In J. L. Nelson, S. B. Palonsky, & M. R. McCarthy, *Critical issues in education.* 6th ed. Boston: McGraw Hill, 2007, p. 227.

References

Gardner, H. (1993). *Frames of mind.* New York: Basic Books. In J. L. Nelson, S. B. Palonsky, & M. R. McCarthy, *Critical issues in education.* 6th ed. Boston: McGraw Hill, 2007, p. 230.

Gardner, H. (2011). *The unschooled mind: How children think and how schools* should *teach.* New York: Basic Books.

Gewertz, C. (2010, February 23). Experts lay out vision for future assessments: More-analytical tasks would replace factual recall of multiple-choice. *Education Week* 29, no 23, p. 8. http://www.edweek.org/ew/articles/2010/02/23/23assessment.h29.html.

Goddard, R. G., Hoy, W. K., & Woolfolk-Hoy, A. (2004). Collective efficacy: Theoretical developments, empirical evidence, and future directions. *Educational Researcher* 33, pp. 3–13.

Gonzalez, N., Moll, L., and Amanti, C., eds. (2005). *Funds of knowledge: Theorizing practice in households, communities, and classrooms.* Mahwah, NJ: Lawrence Erlbaum. In A. W. Boykin & P. Noguera, *Creating the opportunity to learn: Moving from research to practice to close the achievement gap.* Alexandria, VA: ASCD, 2011, pp. 103–4.

Good, C., Aronson, J., & Inzlicht, M. (2003). Improving adolescents' standardized test performance: An intervention to reduce the effects of stereotype threat. *Journal of Applied Developmental Psychology* 24, no. 6. In A. W. Boykin and P. Noguera, *Creating the opportunity to learn: Moving from research to practice to close the achievement gap.* Alexandria, VA: ASCD, 2011, pp. 66–67.

Greenwood, C. R. (1996). Research on the practices and behavior of effective teachers at the Juniper Gardens Children's Project: Implications for the education of diverse learners. In *Research on classroom ecologies: Implications for inclusion of children with learning disabilities*, edited by D. Speech and K. B. Keogh, pp. 39–68. Hillsdale, NJ: Lawrence Erlbaum. In A. W. Boykin and P. Noguera, *Creating the opportunity to learn: Moving from research to practice to close the achievement gap.* Alexandria, VA: ASCD, 2011.

Hale, J. E. (2004). How schools shortchange African American children. *Educational Leadership* 62, no. 3, 34–37. In A. W. Boykin and P. Noguera, *Creating the opportunity to learn: Moving from research to practice to close the achievement gap.* Alexandria, VA: ASCD, 2011, pp. 110–11.

Hallinger, P., and Murphy, J. (1986). The social context of effective schools. *American Journal of Education* 94, no. 3, 328–55. In M. M. Kirby and M. F. DiPaola, *Academic optimism and achievement: A path model.* In W. K. Hoy & M. F. DiPaola, *Studies in school improvement.* Charlotte: Information Age Publishing, 2009.

Hansen, J. (1980). The effects of inference training and practice on young children's comprehension. *Reading Research Quarterly* 16, no. 3, 391–417. In A. W. Boykin and P. Noguera, *Creating the opportunity to learn: Moving from research to practice to close the achievement gap.* Alexandria, VA: ASCD, 2011, pp. 132–33.

Heitin, L. (2012). Flattening the school walls. *Education Week.* http://www.edweek.org/tm/articles/2012/04/18/projbased_or.html

Henderson, A. T., and Mapp, K. L. (2002). *A new wave of evidence: The impact of school, family, and community connections on student achievement.* Austin, TX. Southwest Educational Development Laboratory, National Center for Family & Community Connections with Schools. In M. M. Kirby and M. F. DiPaola, *Academic optimism and achievement: A path model.* In W. K. Hoy & M. F. DiPaola, *Studies in school improvement.* Charlotte: Information Age Publishing, p. 89.

Henderson, N., and Milstein, M. M. (2003). *Resiliency in schools: Making it happen for students and educators.* Thousands Oaks, CA: Corwin Press, Inc.

Horatio Alger Association of Distinguished Americans. (2005). *The state of our nation's youth.* Alexandria, VA: Author. http://www.horatioalger.com/pdfs/stateo5.pdf.

Hoy, W. K., and DiPaola, M. F. (2009). *Studies in school improvement.* Charlotte: Information Age Publishing.

Hoy, W. K., and Hannum, J. W. (1997). Middle school climate: An empirical assessment of organizational health and student achievement. *Educational Administration Quarterly* 33, no. 3, 290–311. In M. M. Kirby and M. F. DiPaola, *Academic optimism and achievement: A path model.* In W. K. Hoy & M. F. DiPaola, *Studies in school improvement.* Charlotte: Information Age Publishing, 2009.

References

Hoy, W. K., Hannum, J. W., and Tschannen-Moran, M. (1998). Organizational climate and student achievement: A parsimonious and longitudinal view. *Journal of School Leadership* 8, 336–59. In M. M. Kirby and M. F. DiPaola, *Academic optimism and achievement: A path model*. In W. K. Hoy & M. F. DiPaola, *Studies in school improvement.* Charlotte: Information Age Publishing, 2009.

Hoy, W. K., Tarter, C. J., and Woolfolk-Hoy, A. (2007). Academic optimism of schools: A force for student achievement. In W. K. Hoy and M. F. DiPaola, eds., *Studies in school improvement.* Charlotte: Information Age Publishing, 2009.

Irvine, J. J. (1990). *Black children and school failure: Policies, practices and prescriptions.* Westport, CT: Greenwood Press. In A. W. Boykin & P. Noguera, *Creating the opportunity to learn: Moving from research to practice to close the achievement gap.* Alexandria, VA: ASCD, 2011, p. 76.

Kagan, S. (1992). *Cooperative learning.* San Clemente, CA: Kagan Cooperative Learning. In W. Boykin and P. Noguera, *Creating the opportunity to learn: Moving from research to practice to close the achievement gap.* Alexandria, VA: ASCD, 2011.

Kelly, D. M. (1993). *Last chance high: How girls and boys drop in and out of alternative schools.* New Haven: Yale University Press.

King, A. (1992). Facilitating elaborative learning through guided student-generated questioning. *Educational Psychologist* 27, no. 1, 111–26. In A. W. Boykin and P. Noguera, *Creating the opportunity to learn: Moving from research to practice to close the achievement gap.* Alexandria, VA: ASCD, 2011.

Kirby, M. M., and DiPaola, M. F., ed. (2009). *Academic optimism and achievement: A path model.* In W. K. Hoy & M. F. DiPaola, *Studies in school improvement.* Charlotte: Information Age Publishing.

Krovetz, M., and Arriaza, G. (2006). *Collaborative teacher leadership: How teachers can foster equitable schools.* Thousand Oaks, CA. Corwin Press. In C. Dean and D. Parsley, Changing schools: Re-imagine high performance. *Success in Sight Module 4: School Culture & Change: Leveraging the Power of Productive Mindsets*, 2011, p. 2.

Ladd, G. W., Birch, S. H., and Buhs, E. S. (1999). Children's social and scholastic lives in kindergarten: Related spheres of influence? *Child Development* 70, no. 6, 1373–1400. In A. W. Boykin and P. Noguera, *Creating the opportunity to learn: Moving from research to practice to close the achievement gap.* Alexandria, VA: ASCD, 2011, p. 77.

Ladson-Billings, G. (1995). Toward a theory of culturally relevant pedagogy. *American Educational Research Journal* 32, no. 3, 465–506. In W. Boykin and P. Noguera, *Creating the opportunity to learn: Moving from research to practice to close the achievement gap.* Alexandria, VA: ASCD, 2011, p. 102.

Ladson-Billings, G. (2002). But that's just good teaching! The case for culturally relevant pedagogy. In S. J. Denbo and L. M. Beaulieu, eds., *Improving schools for African American students: A reader for educational leaders*, pp. 95–102. Springfield, IL: Charles C. Thomas.

LAO. (2007). In P. Warren, P. (2007). *Improving alternative education in California.* California Legislative Analyst's Office (LAO). http://www.lao.ca.gov/2007/alternative_educ/alt_ed_020707.aspx.

Lee, C. D. (2001). Is October Brown Chinese? A cultural modeling activity system for underachieving students. *American Educational Research Journal* 38, no. 1, 97–141. In A. W. Boykin & P. Noguera, *Creating the opportunity to learn: Moving from research to practice to close the achievement gap.* Alexandria, VA: ASCD, 2011.

Lee, C. D. (2006). "Every good-bye ain't gone": Analyzing the cultural underpinnings of classroom talk. *Qualitative Studies in Education* 19, no. 3, 305–27. In A. W. Boykin and P. Noguera, *Creating the opportunity to learn: Moving from research to practice to close the achievement gap.* Alexandria, VA: ASCD, 2011.

Lee, V. E., Smith, J. B., Perry, T. E., and Smylie, M. A. (1999). *Social support, academic press, and student achievement.* Chicago: Consortium on Chicago School Research. In M. M. Kirby and M. F. DiPaola, *Academic optimism and achievement: A path model.* In W. K. Hoy & M. F. DiPaola, *Studies in school improvement.* Charlotte: Information Age Publishing, 2009.

References

Lehr, C. A., Lanners, E. J., and Lange, C. M. (2003). Alternative schools: Policy and legislation across the United States. (Research Report 1). Institute on Community Integration (UCEDD): The College of Education & Human Development: University of Minnesota.

Linnenbrink, E. A., and Pintrich, P. R. (2003). The role of self-efficacy beliefs in student engagement and learning in the classroom. *Reading and Writing Quarterly: Overcoming Learning Difficulties* 19, no. 2, 119–37.

Lundsgaard, N., ed. (2004 April). Rigor: What does it mean to you? *Focus* 3, no. 9.

Lynch, D. J. (2008). Confronting challenges: Motivational beliefs and learning strategies in difficult college courses. *College Student Journal* 42, 416–21.

Maheady, L., Mallette, B., Harper, G. F., and Sacca, K. (1991). Heads together: A peer-mediated option for improving the academic achievement of heterogeneous learning groups. *Remedial and Special Education* 12, no. 2, 25–33. In W. Boykin and P. Noguera, *Creating the opportunity to learn: Moving from research to practice to close the achievement gap.* Alexandria, VA: ASCD, 2011.

Mayers, P. L. (July, 1978). Flow in adolescence and its relation to school experience. *Dissertation Abstracts International* 39(1-A), 197–98. In Gilman, Huebner, & Furlong, eds., 2009.

McREL. (2011). Re-imagine high performance. *Changing Schools* 64 (Fall), 1–13. doi: ISSN 2150-1106.

Molden, D. C., and Dweck, C. S. (2006). Finding "meaning" in psychology: A lay theories approach to self-regulation, social perception, and social development. *American Psychologist* 61, no. 3, 192–203. In W. Boykin and P. Noguera, *Creating the opportunity to learn: Moving from research to practice to close the achievement gap.* Alexandria, VA: ASCD, 2011.

Mueller, C. M., and Dweck, C. S. (1998). Praise for intelligence can undermine children's motivation and performance, *Journal of Personality and Social Psychology* 75, no. 1, 33–52. In A. W. Boykin and P. Noguera, *Creating the opportunity to learn: Moving from research to practice to close the achievement gap.* Alexandria, VA: ASCD, 2011.

Nakamura, J. (1988). Optimal experiences and the uses of talent. In Csikszentmihalyi and Csikszentmihalyi, eds., 1988.

Nelson, J. L., Palonsky, S. B., and McCarthy, M. R. (2007). *Critical issues in education.* 6th ed. Boston: McGraw Hill.

Newby, T. J. (1991). Classroom motivation: Strategies of first-year teachers. *Journal of Educational Psychology* 83, no. 2, 195–200. In A. W. Boykin and P. Noguera, *Creating the opportunity to learn: Moving from research to practice to close the achievement gap.* Alexandria, VA: ASCD, 2011, pp. 91–92.

New Mexico Center for Dispute Resolution. (n.d.). http://www.unm.edu/~pamo/dispute.htm.

No Child Left Behind Act of 2001. Reauthorization of the elementary and secondary education act: Reauthorization of the elementary and secondary education act, public law: 107-110 (H. R. 1) (January 8, 2002).

Noddings, N. (1995). A morally defensible mission for schools in the 21st century. *Kappan* 76: 365–6. In J. L. Nelson, S. B. Palonsky, & M. R. McCarthy, *Critical issues in education.* 6th ed. Boston: McGraw Hill, 2007, p. 8.

Noddings, N. (2003). *Happiness and education.* Cambridge, NY: Cambridge University Press.

Oxley, D. (1994). Organizing schools into small units: Alternatives to homogeneous grouping. *Phi Delta Kappan* 75, no. 7, 521–26. In M. N. C. Wang, G. D. Haertel, and H. J. Walberg, Educational resilience in inner cities. In M. C. Wang & E. Gordon, eds., *Educational resilience in inner-city America: Challenges and prospects,* pp. 45–72. Hillsdale, NJ: Erlbaum, 1996.

Paredes, V. (1991). *School climate and student achievement.* Austin Independent School District. http://eric.ed.gov/ERICDocs/data/ericdocs2sql/content_storage_01/00000196/823/38/68.pdf.

Parrett, W. H., and Budge, K. M. (2012). *Turning high-poverty schools into high-performing schools.* Alexandria, Virginia: ASCD.

Ruiz de Velasco, J. The Earl Warren Institute, University of California, Berkeley. (April, 2008). *Alternative education in continuation high schools: Meeting the needs of over-aged under-credited youth.* Berkeley: Boalt Hall School of Law.

Ruiz de Velasco, J., and McLaughlin, M. University of California Berkeley, School of Law and the John W. Gardner Center for Youth and Their Communities (JGC). (2012). *Raising the bar, building capacity: Driving improvement in California continuation high schools.*

Ryan, R., and Deci, E. L. (2000). Self-determination theory and the facilitation of intrinsic motivation, social development, and well-being. *American Psychologist* 55, no. 1, 68–78.

Ryan, R., and Deci, E. L. (2006). Self-regulation and the problem of human autonomy: Does psychology need choice, self-determination, and will? *Journal of Personality* 74, no. 6, 1557–86, in A. W. Boykin and P. Noguera, *Creating the opportunity to learn: Moving from research to practice to close the achievement gap.* Alexandria, VA: ASCD, 2011, p. 84.

Rychlak, J. F. (1976). *Dialectic.* Basil, Switzerland: Karger. In J. L. Nelson, S. B. Palonsky, & M. R. McCarthy, *Critical issues in education.* 6th ed. Boston: McGraw Hill, 2007, p. 8.

Sadowski, M., ed. (2004). *Teaching immigrant and second-language students.* Cambridge, MA: Harvard University Press. In W. H. Parrett and K. M. Budge, *Turning high-poverty schools into high-performing schools.* Alexandria, Virginia: ASCD, 2012, p. 127.

Schneider, B., and Bowen, D. E. (1995). *Winning the service game.* Boston: Harvard Business School.

Schneider, B., White, S. S., and Paul, M. C. (1998). Linking service climate and customer perceptions of service quality: Test of a causal model. *Journal of Applied Psychology* 83, no. 2, 150–63.

Schunk, D. H. (2003). Self-efficacy for reading and writing: Influence of modeling, goal setting, and self-evaluation. *Reading and Writing Quarterly* 19, no. 2, 159–72. In A. W. Boykin and P. Noguera, *Creating the opportunity to learn: Moving from research to practice to close the achievement gap.* Alexandria, VA: ASCD, 2011.

Schunk, D. H., and Zimmerman, B. J. (2007). Influencing children's self-efficacy and self-regulation of reading and writing through modeling. *Reading and Writing Quarterly* 23, no. 1, 7–25.

Sciabarra, C. M. (1999). *Ayn Rand: The Russian radical.* University Park: Pennsylvania State University Press. In J. L. Nelson, S. B. Palonsky, and M. R. McCarthy, *Critical issues in education.* 6th ed. Boston: McGraw Hill, 2007, p. 16.

Seifert, T. L. (2004). Understanding student motivation. *Educational Research*, 46, no. 2, 137–49.

Seligman, M. E. (2006). *Learned optimism: How to change your mind and your life.* New York: Vintage Books.

Shell, D. F., & Husman, J. (2008). Control, motivation, affect, and strategic self-regulation in the college classroom: A multidimensional phenomenon. *Journal of Educational Psychology* 100, no. 2, 443–59.

Sim, M. (1999). *From puzzles to principles?* Lanham, MD: Lexington Books.

Skinner, E. A., and Belmont, M. J. (1993). Motivation in the classroom: Reciprocal effects of teacher behavior and student engagement across the school year. *Journal of Educational Psychology* 85, no. 4, 571–81. In A. W. Boykin and P. Noguera, *Creating the opportunity to learn: Moving from research to practice to close the achievement gap.* Alexandria, VA: ASCD, 2011.

Stevens, T., Olivarez, A., and Hamman, D. (2006). The role of cognition, motivation, and emotion in explaining the mathematics achievement gap between Hispanic and white students. *Hispanic Journal of Behavioral Sciences* 28, no. 2, 161.

Stewart, E. (2008). Family- and individual-level predictors of academic success for African American students: A longitudinal path analysis utilizing national data. *Journal of Black Studies* 36, no. 4. In A. W. Boykin and P. Noguera, *Creating the opportunity to learn: Moving from research to practice to close the achievement gap.* Alexandria, VA: ASCD, 2011, p. 72.

Stiggins, R., and DuFour, R. (2009). Maximizing the power of formative assessments. *Phi Delta Kappan* 90, no. 9. In W. H. Parrett and K. M. Budge, *Turning high-poverty schools into high-performing schools.* Alexandria, Virginia: ASCD, 2012, pp. 164–65.

Thernstrom, A., and Thernstrom, S. (2003). *No excuses. Closing the racial gap in learning.* New York: Simon & Schuster.

Tucker, C., Zayco, R., Herman, K., Reinke, W., Trujillo, M., Carraway, K., Wallack, C. and Ivery, P. (2002). Teacher and child variables as predictors of academic engagement among low-income African American children. *Psychology in the Schools* 39, no. 4, 477–88. In A. W. Boykin and P. Noguera, *Creating the opportunity to learn: Moving from research to practice to close the achievement gap*. Alexandria, VA: ASCD, 2011, p. 76.

Turner, J. C., Meyer, D. K., Anderman, E. M., Midgley, C., Gheen, M., Yongjin, K., and Patrick, H. (2002). The classroom environment and students' reports of avoidance strategies in mathematics: A multimethod study. *Journal of Educational Psychology* 94, no. 1, 88–106. In A. W. Boykin and P. Noguera, *Creating the opportunity to learn: Moving from research to practice to close the achievement gap*. Alexandria, VA: ASCD, 2011, p. 47.

Tzafrir, S. S., & Gur, A. B. A. (2007). HRM practices and perceived service quality: The role of trust as a mediator. Research and Practice in Human Resource Management 15, no. 2, 1–20.

Urquhart, V. (2011). Q & A: Focus on high expectations has lasting impact. In *Changing schools: Re-imagine high performance*. McREL (f)2011.

U.S. Census Bureau. (2000). In J. L. Nelson, S. B. Palonsky, and M. R. McCarthy, *Critical issues in education*. 6th ed. Boston: McGraw Hill, 2007, pp. 200–6.

U.S. Department of Education, Office of Planning, Evaluation and Policy Development. (2010). *ESEA Blueprint for Reform*, Washington, DC.

Vansteenkiste, M., Lens, W., and Deci, E. L. (2006). Intrinsic versus extrinsic goal contents in self-determination theory: Another look at the quality of academic motivation. *Educational Psychologist* 41, no. 1, 19–31. In A. W. Boykin and P. Noguera, *Creating the opportunity to learn: Moving from research to practice to close the achievement gap*. Alexandria, VA: ASCD, 2011, p. 85.

Vansteenkiste, M., and Sheldon, K. M. (2006). There's nothing more practical than a good theory: Integrating motivational interviewing and self-determination theory. *British Journal of Clinical Psychology* 45, no. 1, 63–82. In A. W. Boykin and P. Noguera, *Creating the opportunity to learn: Moving from research to practice to close the achievement gap*. Alexandria, VA: ASCD, 2011, p. 85.

Wang, M. N. C., Haertel, G. D., & Walberg, H. J. (1994). Educational resilience in inner cities. In M. C. Wang & E. Gordon, eds., *Educational resilience in inner-city America: Challenges and prospects*, pp. 45–72. Hillsdale, NJ: Erlbaum.

Ware, F. (2006). Warm demander pedagogy: Culturally responsible teaching that supports a culture of achievement for African American students. *Urban Education* 41, no. 4, 427–56. In A. W. Boykin and P. Noguera, *Creating the opportunity to learn: Moving from research to practice to close the achievement gap*. Alexandria, VA: ASCD, 2011, p. 76.

Warren, P. (2007). *Improving alternative education in California*. California Legislative Analyst's Office (LAO). http://www.lao.ca.gov/2007/alternative_educ/alt_ed_020707.aspx.

Warring, W. H. (2011). *Resiliency in at-risk high school students: Why and how some succeed*. (Published doctoral dissertation, Argosy University). http://search.proquest.com/pqdt/advanced.

Waters, T. (2011). *Changing schools: Reimagine high performance*. McREL 64 (Fall 2011), p. 1A.

Weiner, B. (2000). Intrapersonal and interpersonal theories of motivation from an attributional perspective. *Educational Psychology Review* 12, no. 1, 1–14. In W. Boykin and P. Noguera, *Creating the opportunity to learn: Moving from research to practice to close the achievement gap*. Alexandria, VA: ASCD, 2011.

Werner, E. E., and Smith, R. S. (1992). *Overcoming the odds: High risk children from birth to adulthood*. Ithaca, NY: Cornell University Press.

Wheat, C. (2009). The silence in failing schools. *Education Services Australia*. http://www.eqa.edu.au/site/thesilenceinfailing.html.

Wolk, R. A. (2011). *Wasting minds: Why our education system is failing and what we can do about it*. Alexandria, VA: ASDC.

Zigarelli, M. A. (1996). An empirical test of conclusions from effective schools research. *Journal of Educational Research* 90, 103–10. In M. M. Kirby and M. F. DiPaola, *Academic optimism and achievement: A path model. In* W. K. Hoy & M. F. DiPaola, *Studies in school improvement.* Charlotte: Information Age Publishing, 2009.

Index

ability, 12
academic motivators, 45
academic optimism, 19, 40, 52, 63, 69
Academic Optimism and Achievement: A Path Model (Kirby and DiPaola), 63
academic press, 14, 40
Accelerated Middle Schools, 61
Achievement for Latinos through Academic Success (ALAS), 61
adaptive learning strategies, 74, 75
Adolescent and School Health, 45
adult stakeholders, trusting, 20–23
adversity, 1–2; efficacious moments and events and, 4–5; overcoming struggles and, 2–3; self-debasement and, 3–4; summary of, 5–6
affective engagement, 71, 72
ALAS. *See* Achievement for Latinos through Academic Success
Almeida, C., 87, 88
Amanti, C., 57
Anand, P. G., 77
apathy, 11, 46
Aronson, J., 41, 42
Arriaza, G., 21
assessments, 87, 105; demonstrating tools and strategies for, 92; dominant consorts and, 87–90; performance-based, 27, 88–89; predicting student struggles and, 90–91; of student growth, 31–34; of student performance, 91–92; summary of, 92–93; summative, 25; test-taking, 89
asset-focused factors, 58, 72, 73
assets, 26–27
at-risk factors, 9
attitudes, 2, 3
attribution theory, 10–14, 17
autonomy, 74–76
avoidance strategies, 72

Baldwin, James, 104
Balfanz, R., 90, 93
Bamburg, A., 20, 21
Bandura, A., 42
behavioral engagement, 71
belief systems, 11
Belmont, M. J., 72
benign neglect, x, 8
Birch, S. H., 51
black students, 51–52
blame game, 10–14
Bodovski, K. J., 71
Boston Compact, 16, 17
Boston Private Industry Council, 16
Bowen, D. E., 19
Boykin, A. W., 12, 40, 50, 51, 57, 73, 75
Bridgeland, J. M., 22, 49, 90, 93
Brock, William, 10
Brookover, W. B., 40
Bruce, M., 90, 93
Budge, K. M., 9, 56

117

Buhs, E. S., 51
Burke-Morison, K., 49
business: needs, 9; paradigms, 16
Business Roundtable, 16, 17

California Department of Education, ix
Career Academies, 61–62
career opportunities, 10
Career Technical Education (CTE), 67
Carraway, K., 51
Casteel, C., 51
CCSS. *See* Common Core State Standard Initiative
CCSSO. *See* Council of Chief State School Officers
CDC. *See* Centers for Disease Control and Prevention
Census Bureau, U.S., 10
Centers for Disease Control and Prevention (CDC), 45
Cervantes, R., 87
Chan, L. K. S., 42
Character Education Partnership, 15
choice, 28, 53, 67; pedagogical, 25; responsible, 24; self-efficacy and, 23; student growth and, 23; trusting, 23–25
civic learning, 101
classroom engagement, 71–73; effective teaching approaches for, 82–83; flow and, 78–80; personalizing instruction and, 77–78; restructuring curriculum and, 80–82; self-determination and, 74–76; summary of, 83–84
classwide peer tutoring (CWPT), 58
coercion, 24
cognitive elaboration, 74, 75
Coleman Report, 40
collective efficacy, 40
college and career readiness, 29; assessing growth and, 31–34; CCSS and, 30–31; requirement indicators and, 29–30; summary of, 34–35
collegiality, 20
Common Core State Standard Initiative (CCSS), 29, 30, 30–31, 34, 96
community-based issues, 57
community-based projects, 81
competition, 15; foreign labor, 10
Comprehensive School Reform model, 64

conflict: cultural, 9–10, 16–17; generational, 16, 17
conflict-resolution programs, 65–66
connectedness, 45–46, 53
Conoley, C. W., 79
Conoley, J. C., 79
contextual influences, 44
control, 11
Cordova, D. I., 78
corporate needs, 9–10
Council for Corporate and School Partnerships, 16, 17
Council of Chief State School Officers (CCSSO), 29, 88
credit points, 8
critical consciousness, 23
critical incidents, 4, 5
critical literacy, 23
critical thinking, 68
Csikszentmihalyi, M., 78
CTE. *See* Career Technical Education
culture: conflict and, 9–10, 16–17; diversity and, 51; of family, 13; of school, 14–16; values and, 56
curriculum: design, 67–68, 69; restructuring, 80–82, 84; student-engaging, 42
curriculum-based learning, 8
CWPT. *See* classwide peer tutoring

Dallmann-Jones, A., 48
debates, 78
Department of Education, U.S., 48, 88
Developing and Assessing School Culture: A New Level of Accountability for Schools (Character Education Partnership), 15
dialectic reasoning, 59, 60, 69
dialogue, 60
Dianda, M. R., 61
Dickens, Charles, 97
Dilulio, J. J., 49
DiPaola, M. F., 40, 63
disrespect, 7, 8
dualistic thoughts, 60
DuFour, R., 90, 93
Dweck, C. S., 41, 42
dysfunctionality, 43

earning, 7
Edmonds, R. R., 40
Education Week, 42
efficacy, 1; collective, 40; moments and events of, 4–5; self-efficacy, 4, 14, 23, 58, 63, 69
effort, 2, 12
Eliot, Charles W., 44
Ellis, A., 1, 4, 5, 26
emotional drives, 11
emotional feedback, 73
enterprises, 81
entry points, 78; esthetic, 78; experiential, 78; foundational, 78; logical-quantitative, 78; narrational, 78
esthetic entry points, 78
experiential entry points, 78
external attribution, 11

faculty collegiality, 20
family culture, 13
Farkas, G., 71
fear, 43
field experts, ix
Fire in the Ashes (Kozol), 89
fixed views, 41
"Flattening the School Walls" (Heitin), 42
flow, 78–80
foreign labor competition, 10
foundational entry points, 78
Free Schools (Kozol), 89
Fried, C., 42
Friere, P., 23

Gardner, H., 23, 45, 78, 82, 83
generational conflict, 16, 17
Gewertz, C., 88
Gonzalez, N., 57
Good, C., 41, 42
Greenwood, C. R., 71

Haertel, G. D., 44, 49, 60, 81
Hallinger, P., 40
Hansen, J., 75, 76
Harper, R. A., 1, 4, 5, 26
Harvard University, 44
Heitin, Liana, 42, 43
Henderson, A. T., 63
Henderson, N., 65, 66

Herman, R., 51
highly toxic environment, 43
Hispanic families, 13
home visits, 56, 68
Horatio Alger Association of Distinguished Americans, 76
Horn, Tom, 42, 43
Hornig-Fox, J., 90, 93
Houseman, A. E., 103
Hoy, W. K., 14
Hughes, Langston, 33
Husman, J., 42

implicit theories, 12
individualized graduation plans, 46
inferential learning, 76
information-processing quality, 73
instructional design criteria, 62–64
instructional influences, 44
intelligence, , 41; multiple, 23
interactive collegiality, 20
internal attribution, 11
Internet, 96
internships, 81
intersubjectivity, 73
interventions, 55–; instructional design criteria and, 62–64; methodologies and, 59–62; Multiple Pathways approach to curriculum design and, 67–68; student misbehavior strategies and, 65–66; summary of, 68–69; targeted, 39
Inzlicht, M., 41
Irvine, J. J., 51
Ivery, P., 51

Jackson, 58
Jobs for America's Graduates (JAG), 62
job training, 68

Kelly, Deidra, ix
King, A., 75
King, Martin Luther, Jr., 92
Kirby, M. M., 40, 63
Kozol, Jonathan, 89
Krovetz, M., 21

labor: foreign competition, 10; outsourcing, 10
Ladd, G. W., 51

Ladson-Billings, G., 57
Lange, C. M., x, xiv
language, 102
Lanners, E. J., x, xiv
LAO. *See* Legislative Analyst's Office
Latino students, 51–52
laziness, 9
Le, C., 87
learning: adaptive strategies for, 74, 75; civic, 101; communities, 62; curriculum-based, 8; inferential, 76; project-based, 42–; rigorous, 81; self-regulated, 58
Lee, C. D., 74
Lee, Harper, 31
Legislative Analyst's Office (LAO), ix
Lehr, C. A., x, xiv
Lepper, M. R., 78
Letter from a Birmingham Jail (King, M. L., Jr.), 92
Lezotte, L. W., 40
linkage research, 19
Linnenbring, E. A., 42
literature, 103
logical-quantitative entry points, 78
London, Jack, 97
Lundsgaard, N., 81–82, 82
Lynch, D. J., 42

Mapp, K. L., 63
Mason County School District, 56
McCarthy, M. R., 15, 17, 42, 43, 59, 60, 81
McLaughlin, M., 62, 90
media, 96
Meier, Deborah, 89
mentoring: peer, 58; technical, 81
methodologies, 59–62
Middle College High Schools, 62
Milstein, M. M., 65, 66
Mizer, Jean, 46
Molden, D. C., 42
Moll, L., 57
monistic thoughts, 60
Moore, P. J., 42
motivation, 10, 11, 26; academic motivators, 45; flow and, 78–80
Mueller, C. M., 41
multiple intelligences, 23

Multiple Pathways approach, to curriculum design, 67–68, 69
Murphy, J., 40

narrational entry points, 78
National Education Association, 61
National Governors Association (NGA), 29, 88
national honor societies, 14
NCLB. *See* No Child Left Behind
Nelson, J. L., 15, 16, 17, 42, 43, 59, 60, 81
Newby, T. J., 82
New Chance, 62
NGA. *See* National Governors Association
No Child Left Behind (NCLB), 16, 88
Noddings, N., , 8, 24, 25, 44
Noguera, P., 12, 40, 50, 51, 57, 73, 75
Numbered Heads Together, 58
"On a Roll" program, 65

on-task behaviors, 71
outcomes, 26–27; performance, 12
outsourcing, 10
Oxley, D., 49

Palonsky, S. B., 15, 17, 42, 43, 59, 60, 81
parents, 55
Parrett, W. H., 9, 56
Paul, M. C., 19
pedagogical choice, 25
peer mentoring, 58
performance-based assessments, 27, 88–89
performance outcomes, 12
personalization: of instruction, 77–78, 84; of teacher attributes, 49
Pintrich, P. R., 42
points, 8; entry, 78
preparation books, 92
primary sources, 96
Process of Conflict Mediation, 66
profit, 30
program design, 42–43
project-based learning, 42–
protective factors, xiii, 1, 5, 45–46, 53
"Protective Factors and School Connectedness" (CDC), 45
psychological influences, 44
Public Agenda, 89

Quantum Opportunity Program, 62

racial background, 51
racial bias, 89–
Reinke, W., 51
relevance, 14, 82, 84
resiliency, xiii, 4, 15, 95; attitudes and, 3; flow and, 79; mind-sets and, 6
respect, 28; control and, 11; disrespect, 7, 8; self-respect, 41; trust and, 25–26
responsibility, 23, 28
responsible choice, 24
rigidly applied algorithms,
rigor, 14, 67
rigorous learning, 81
roadblocks, 7–8; attribution theory and, 10–14; cultural conflict and, 9–10; school culture and, 14–16; for school design, 43–44; summary of, 16–17
Ross, S. M., 77
Ruiz de Velasco, J., 62, 90

Safety Net quality, ix
Schneider, B., 19
school climate, 40
school culture, 14–16
school design, 39–42; connectedness and, 45–46; program design and, 42–43; questioning, 44–45; roadblocks and challenges for, 43–44; strengthening teaching and, 49–52; student needs and, 46–47; summary of, 52–53
Schunk, D. H., 39, 72
secondary sources, 96
Seifert, T. L., 42
self-debasement, 3–4, 8
self-determination, 74–76, 83
self-efficacy, 4, 14, 23, 58, 63, 69
self-esteem, 1, 11, 65
self-images, 23
self-improvement, 40–
self-reflection, 32
self-regulated learning, 58
self-respect, 41
self-serving attribution, 11
Seligman, M. E., 11
Sem Yeto High School, ix, x
SES. *See* socioeconomical status
Shadow Child Syndrome, 48

The Shame of the Nation (Kozol), 89
Sheldon, K. M., 74
Shell, D. F., 42
Sizer, Theodore, 89
Skinner, E. A., 72
small unit schools, 49
Smith, R. S., 1
social exchanges, 73
socioeconomical status (SES), 40
standardized testing, , 88, 90
Steinberg, A., 87
Stevens, T., 73
Stewart, E., 73
Stiggins, R., 90, 93
student-engaging curriculum, 42
student growth, 8; assessing, 31–34; choice and, 23; development of, 26–27
student misbehavior strategies, 65–66
student performance, assessing, 91–92
students: black, 51–52; desire of, 67; engagement of, 58, 68; interest of, 67; Latino, 51–52; needs of, 46–47; predicting struggles of, 90–91; wants of, 45, 53
subject matter exposure, 24
summative assessments, 25
synthesized economies, 10

Talent Development High Schools, 62
targeted interventions, 39
Tarter, C. J., 14
taxpayers, 96
teacher perception, 72
Teacher-Student Relationship Quality (TSRQ), 50–51, 51–52
teaching, strengthening of, 49–52
technical mentoring, 81
test-taking assessment, 89
Thernstrom, A., 89, 93
Thernstrom, S., 89, 93
thought, 30; dualistic, 60; frameworks, 1, 5; monistic, 60
To Kill a Mockingbird (Lee), 31
Trujillo, W., 51
trust, 19–22, 40, 56, 103; of adult stakeholders, 20–23; of choice, 23–25; respect and, 25–26; student growth development and, 26–27; summary of, 27–28

trust-to-choose model, x
TSRQ. *See* Teacher-Student Relationship Quality
Tucker, C., 51
"Using Computer-Assisted Instruction to Personalize Arithmetic Materials for Elementary School Children" (Anand and Ross), 77

Vansteenkiste, M., 74
virtual apprenticeships, 81
vocabulary, 102
vocational programs, 44

Walberg, H. J., 44, 49, 60, 81
Wallack, C., 51

Wang, M. N. C., 44, 49, 60, 81
wants, of students, 45, 53
Ware, F., 51
warm-demander pedagogy, 51
Waters, T., 14
Werner, E. E., 1
Wheat, C., 80
"When I Was One and Twenty" (Houseman),
White, S. S., 19
Wilhoit, Gene, 88
Wolk, R. A., , 49, 68, 76, 88, 89

Zayco, R., 51
Zimmerman, B. J., 72

About the Author

William H. Warring, Jr., Ed.D

    The author is retired from a twenty-year teaching career with service in high school continuation education as well as middle school comprehensive and opportunity programs.
    His work in making California's English-Language Arts state standard curricula relevant to the wants and needs of continuation students led to teacher-of-the-year awards from both his school and school district. Distinguished service nods from the Solano County Office of Education and the

California Department of Education, were preceded by adjunct positions with Sonoma State University and Touro University Colleges of Education.

Dr. Warring's service with the California Continuation Education Association (CCEA) led to his appointment as a *model school* "field expert" by the California Department of Education (CDE). The author joins other CCEA officials in visiting California continuation schools each year to determine those qualified to receive the CDE's coveted "Model School" award. He currently serves as vice-president of the CCEA.

Previous works by the author include: *Gramma Sandy Wants to Help: a classroom discipline problem-solving program for grades 4- 10* (Front Row Experience, 1994) and *Leaving No Child Behind: A teacher's model for meeting the challenges of the No Child Left Behind Act* (Warring & Associates Publishing, 2008).

www.ingramcontent.com/pod-product-compliance
Lightning Source LLC
Chambersburg PA
CBHW030143240426
43672CB00005B/242